TEACHER'S GUIDE

GUIDED READING PROGRAM

Fiction Focus

2nd Edition

by Gay Su Pinnell
The Ohio State University

and

Irene Fountas
Lesley University

Table of Contents

Table of Contents

USING YOUR
GUIDED READING PROGRAM

The *Scholastic Guided Reading Program* is a varied collection of books that are categorized by the kind and level of challenge they offer children as they are learning to read. The Guided Reading Program consists of 260 books organized into 26 levels of difficulty—Levels A–Z. Many different characteristics of the texts are considered in determining the level of challenge and support a particular book or shorter story presents.

Advantages of a Leveled Book Collection

A leveled book set has many advantages, including the following:

- **It provides experience with a wide variety of texts within a level.**
- **It makes it easier to select books for groups of children.**
- **It lends itself to flexible grouping.**
- **It provides a way to assess children's progress.**
- **It provides a basic book collection that can be expanded over time.**

Multiple Copies of Books	Six copies of each book are provided so that children in small groups will have access to their own copies. Having a collection of books on various levels, with multiple copies of each book, allows you to consider individual strengths when grouping and selecting books. To help you identify a book's level quickly, you may place a Guided Reading Program sticker for the level on the front or back of each book cover.
Flexibility of Use	With a gradient of text, grouping can be more flexible. Children might read only some of the books in a level, and not necessarily in the same sequence. In addition, children may change groups based on individual needs. The **Characteristics of Text** and **Behaviors to Notice and Support**, on pages 80–105, will assist you in placing children in the appropriate levels.
	If you note that some students need extra support for a particular text or that the selection is too difficult for most of the group, you can abandon guided reading and instead use shared reading to experience the book. Then you can select an easier book the next day. As students progress, have them reread books on a lower level for enjoyment. Students will become more confident readers as they reread a book for meaning with no need for problem solving.
Adding to the Guided Reading Program	The Guided Reading Program has been designed with adaptability in mind, so you may add copies of children's and your own favorite books to the library. You may place a Guided Reading Program sticker for the suggested level on each book you add.

Variety Within Levels in the Collection

When working with groups in classroom reading, a broad base of text is needed. The Guided Reading Program provides this broad base. Readers who experience only one kind of book may develop a narrow range of strategies for processing text. With a leveled set, difficulty is controlled because all text characteristics have been factored in. Yet the level of text is not artificially controlled because the variety of text characteristics occurs within natural story language.

The early levels of the Guided Reading Program introduce students to reading print. While reading at these beginning levels, students apply phonics skills, develop a core of high-frequency words, work with print in a variety of layouts, and engage with a variety of high-interest texts.

Books at later levels (Levels J and beyond) include a wider range of text. Within each level, literary texts are included. Essentially, there are three kinds of books at these levels, although there is variety within each category.

- **First, there are picture books at a more sophisticated level than before. These picture books provide an opportunity to expand vocabulary, to interpret stories, and to recognize how illustrations contribute to the story. Like the short story, picture books provide the advanced reader with complex reading material that does not take several days to complete.**

- **Second, there are informational books that are generally shorter. These present complex ideas and some technical language. They challenge students to acquire and discuss ideas and information and to go beyond the text to research topics of interest to them.**

- **Third, there are longer stories and chapter books. These longer selections provide an opportunity for readers to sustain reading over time, remembering details and getting to know characters as they develop.**

FACTORS CONSIDERED IN
LEVELING BOOKS

In placing a book, short story, or article along a gradient of text, multiple characteristics of text are considered. Here is a sample list.

Book and Print Features
Refers to the physical aspects of the text—what readers cope with in terms of length, size, print layout, and font size. It also refers to the interpretation of illustrations and the relationships between information in graphics and the body of the text.

- How many words are in the book?
- How many lines of text are on each page?
- How many pages are in the book?
- What size is the print?
- How much space is there between words and lines?
- How easy is it to find information?
- What is the relationship between print and illustrations?
- Are there graphics (photos, diagrams, maps) that provide essential information and how easy are the graphics to interpret?
- What are the features of print layout? (For example, do sentences begin on the left or do they "wrap around" so that end punctuation must be relied upon?)
- Is print placed in standard, predictable places on the pages or is it used in creative ways that require the reader's flexibility?
- Do the size and shape of book, binding, and layout play a role in text interpretation?

Genre
Means the "type" or "kind" and refers to a classification system formed to provide a way of talking about what texts are like (fiction—including realistic fiction, fantasy, traditional literature; and nonfiction—including biography, autobiography, and informational texts).

- What is the "genre" or "kind" of book?
- What special demands does this genre make on readers?
- Is this an easy or more difficult example of the genre?

Content
Refers to the subject matter that readers are required to understand as they read both fiction and nonfiction texts.

- What background information is essential for understanding this text?
- What new information will readers need to grasp to read the text?
- How accessible is the content to the readers?

Themes and Ideas
Refers to the "big picture," the universality of the problem in the text and its relevance to people's lives.

- What is the theme of the text?
- Are there multiple themes that the reader must understand and be able to talk about?
- How accessible are the "big ideas" to the reader?

Language and Literary Features

Refers to the writer's style and use of literary devices. Literary features are those elements typically used in literature to capture imagination, stir emotions, create empathy or suspense, give readers a sense that the characters and story are real, and make readers care about the outcome of the plot. Nonfiction books may incorporate some literary features.

- From what perspective is the story or informational text written?
- Does the book include devices such as headings, labels, and captions?
- Are graphical elements such as diagrams, tables, charts, and maps included?
- To what degree does the writer use literary language, such as metaphor?
- How easy is it to understand the characters and their motivations and development?
- Is character development essential to the story?
- Is dialogue assigned (using *he said*) or unassigned with longer stretches of interchange that the reader must follow and attribute to one character or another?
- How are characters revealed through what they say or think and what others say or think about them?
- How essential to the story are understandings about setting and plot?

Vocabulary and Words

Refers to the words and their accessibility to readers. Vocabulary generally refers to the meaning of words that readers may decode but not understand. Word solving refers to both decoding and to understanding meaning.

- What is the frequency of multisyllabic words in the text?
- How complex are word meanings? (For example, are readers required to understand multiple meanings or subtle shades of meaning of words?)
- What prior knowledge is needed to understand the vocabulary of the text?
- How many content or technical words are included in the text? How complex are these words?
- Does informational text utilize timeless verb constructions? (Ants *carry* sand as opposed to *carried*.)
- Are generic noun constructions used in informational and/or nonfiction text?

Sentence Complexity

Refers to the syntactic patterns readers will encounter in the text; sentences may be simple (short, with one subject and predicate) or complex (longer, with embedded clauses).

- What is the average length of sentences in the text?
- To what degree do sentences contain embedded clauses?
- What is the sentence style of the writer?
- Are there complex sentences joined by *and, but,* or other conjunctions?
- Are paragraphs organized so that readers can recognize lead sentences and main ideas?

Punctuation

Refers to the graphic symbols that signal the way text should be read to reflect the author's meaning.

- What punctuation symbols are used in the text?
- What do readers need to notice about punctuation in order to fully understand the text?
- What punctuation is essential for readers to notice to read with fluency and phrasing?

Using Leveled Books With Readers

The success of guided reading depends on many factors other than text characteristics. These, of course, have to do with the young readers using the texts as well as teacher-student interactions and include:

- **The reader's prior knowledge of the topic, including vocabulary and concepts.**
- **The reader's prior experience with texts that have similar features.**
- **The way the teacher introduces the text.**
- **The supportive interactions between the teacher and students before, during, and after reading.**
- **The level of interest teachers help students build.**

Level-by-Level Descriptions

Characteristics of text for each level in the Guided Reading Program are listed on pages 80–105. These descriptions are general: not every book included in a level will have every characteristic noted. Also listed are some important behaviors to notice and support at each level. As you use these books with students, you will notice how they support and challenge readers.

Other Resources

You may want to refer to the following resources for descriptions of guided reading as well as additional books for each level:

- **Duke, Nell K., and Bennett-Armistead, V. Susan, 2003.** *Reading & Writing Informational Text in the Primary Grades.* **New York, NY: Scholastic Inc.**
- **Fountas, I. C., and Pinnell, G. S., 2008.** *Benchmark Assessment System 1 and 2.* **Portsmouth, NH: Heinemann.**
- **Fountas, I. C., and Pinnell, G. S., 1996.** *Guided Reading: Good First Teaching for All Children.* **Portsmouth, NH: Heinemann.**
- **Fountas, I. C., and Pinnell, G. S., 2001.** *Guiding Readers and Writers, Grades 3–6: Teaching Comprehension, Genre, and Content Literacy.* **Portsmouth, NH: Heinemann.**
- **Fountas, I. C., and Pinnell, G. S., 2005.** *Leveled Books, K–8: Matching Texts to Readers for Effective Teaching.* **Portsmouth, NH: Heinemann.**
- **Fountas, I. C., and Pinnell, G. S., 1999.** *Voices on Word Matters.* **Portsmouth, NH: Heinemann.**
- **Pinnell, G. S., and Fountas, I. C., 2007.** *The Continuum of Literacy Learning, Grades K–8: Behaviors and Understandings to Notice, Teach, and Support.* **Portsmouth, NH: Heinemann.**
- **Pinnell, G. S., and Fountas, I. C., 1998.** *Word Matters: Teaching Phonics and Spelling in the Reading/Writing Classroom.* **Portsmouth, NH: Heinemann.**
- **Fountas, I. C., and Pinnell, G. S., 2006.** *Teaching for Comprehending and Fluency: Thinking, Talking, and Writing About Reading, K–8.* **Portsmouth, NH: Heinemann.**

WHAT IS
GUIDED READING?

Guided reading is an instructional approach that involves a teacher working with a small group of students who demonstrate similar reading behaviors and can all read similar levels of texts. The text is easy enough for students to read with your skillful support. The text offers challenges and opportunities for problem solving, but is easy enough for students to read with some fluency. You choose selections that help students expand their strategies.

What is the purpose of guided reading?

You select books that students can read with about 90 percent accuracy. Students can understand and enjoy the story because it's accessible to them through their own strategies, supported by your introduction. They focus on meaning but use problem-solving strategies to figure out words they don't know, deal with difficult sentence structure, and understand concepts or ideas they have never before encountered in print.

Why is guided reading important?

Guided reading gives students the chance to apply the strategies they already know to new text. You provide support, but the ultimate goal is independent reading.

When are children ready for guided reading?

Developing readers have already gained important understandings about how print works. These students know how to monitor their own reading. They have the ability to check on themselves or search for possibilities and alternatives if they encounter a problem when reading. For these readers, the guided reading experience is a powerful way to support the development of reading strategies.

The ultimate goal of guided reading is reading a variety of texts with ease and deep understanding. Silent reading means rapid processing of texts with most attention on meaning, which is achieved as readers move past beginning levels (H, I, J). At all levels, students read orally with fluency and phrasing.

Matching Books to Readers

The teacher selects a text for a small group of students who are similar in their reading behaviors at a particular point in time. In general, the text is about right for students in the group. It is not too easy, yet not too hard, and offers a variety of challenges to help readers become flexible problem solvers. You should choose Guided Reading Program books for students that:

- match their knowledge base.
- help them take the next step in learning to read.
- are interesting to them.
- offer just enough challenge to support problem solving while still supporting fluency and meaning.

Supporting Students' Reading

In working with students in guided reading, you constantly balance the difficulty of the text with support for students reading the text. You introduce the story to the group, support individuals through brief interactions while they read, and guide them to talk together afterwards about the words and ideas in the text. In this way, you refine text selection and help individual readers move forward in developing a reading process.

Good readers employ a wide range of word-solving strategies, including analysis of sound-letter relationships and word parts. They must figure out words that are embedded in different kinds of texts. Reading a variety of books enables them to go beyond reading individual words to interpreting language and its subtle meanings.

For more specific teaching suggestions, see individual cards for each book title.

Procedure for Guided Reading

- The teacher works with a small group of students with similar needs.
- The teacher provides introductions to the text that support students' later attempts at problem solving.
- Each student reads the whole text or a unified part of the text.
- Readers figure out new words while reading for meaning.
- The teacher prompts, encourages, and confirms students' attempts at problem solving.
- The teacher and student engage in meaningful conversations about what they are reading.
- The teacher and student revisit the text to demonstrate and use a range of comprehension strategies.

ORGANIZING YOUR CLASSROOM FOR **GUIDED READING**

adapted from *Guided Reading: Making It Work* (Schulman and Payne, 2000)

Good management begins with a thoughtful room arrangement and careful selection of materials; the way you organize furniture and supplies will support the learning that takes place within your classroom. For guided reading to be effective, the rest of the class must be engaged in other literacy activities that do not require direct teacher involvement. For most classes, this means literacy centers that accommodate small groups of students. So, a strategically arranged classroom for guided reading would have a class library, inviting spots for individual work, spaces for whole-class gatherings and small-group meetings, and several literacy centers.

Arranging the room and organizing materials for effective reading and writing workshops takes thought and planning. So before the school year even begins, consider the activities you're planning for your class and the physical layout of your room. With a little ingenuity, you can provide an environment that will support learning all year long.

Scheduling for Guided Reading

To determine the time you'll need for guided reading, consider the number of students in your class and the range of reading abilities they possess. Then create your initial groupings; the ideal group size is four to six, though guided reading groups might range from three to eight. Place below-grade or struggling readers in smaller groups. Keep in mind that sessions are short—often 10–15 minutes for emergent readers, and 15–30 minutes for more advanced readers. You will want to meet with at-risk groups every day; five meetings over a two-week period for more advanced groups is typical. You'll also want to allow yourself some time for assessment—taking a running record, jotting anecdotal notes, or conducting oral interviews, for example. Finally, allow a few minutes between groups to check in with the rest of the class.

THE SCHOLASTIC
GUIDED READING CLASSROOM

Scholastic Guided Reading Programs support a comprehensive reading program by integrating guided instruction, assessment, and independent practice into your classroom. Here's what the Guided Reading classroom looks like:

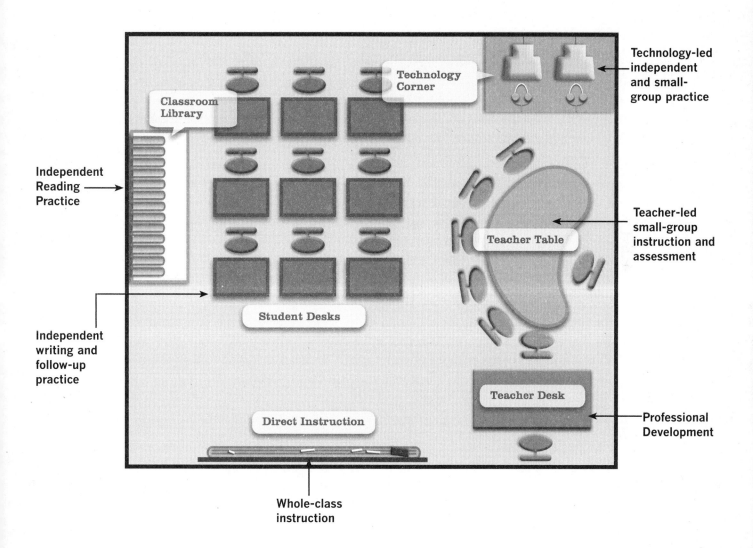

SETTING UP
LITERACY CENTERS

adapted from *Guided Reading: Making It Work* (Schulman and Payne, 2000)

As a way of managing the time to meet with small groups of students, teachers often use literacy centers. At literacy centers, students continue to participate in purposeful and authentic literacy activities. These centers provide many opportunities to practice the skills real readers and writers use. They take the place of traditional worksheets and are not meant to be graded.

Literacy centers can be designed to address a wide range of skill levels, learning styles, and interests. Students work in heterogeneous groups that change often. The number of students at each center depends upon the type of center and the space for it. For example, in one first-grade classroom, the listening center has stations for four students, the computer center accommodates one student per computer, and the library center holds up to three students.

When arranging your centers, consider the number of students you want to accommodate at once, the space you have available, and the topics that you want to cover. Also think about transitions between centers—will students work at the same center during the whole guided reading period? If so, do they know what to do if they finish early? If not, do they know how to move to another center or activity without disturbing you or other class members? Establishing clear expectations and routines will help centers run smoothly, so you can focus on guided reading groups.

When first setting up students' use of literacy centers, take time each day to discuss with students what happened at centers that day. Some questions to consider are, "What went well? What might we change to make it work better?" This helps students think about ways to problem-solve when they meet difficulties working independently.

Things to Consider When Setting Up Literacy Centers

- Establish a manageable number of centers that can be changed easily and routinely.

- Plan time to introduce and demonstrate how each center operates. Some teachers do this during scheduled shared reading/writing time.

- Consider the physical arrangement of the centers to permit movement and a balance of quiet and noisy areas.

- Design centers to meet the range of all learners, addressing a variety of interests and learning styles.

- Have supplies accessible and labeled for independent student use.

- Create signs or charts that communicate functional information and directions, such as "How to Use the Audiocassette Player."

- Develop a plan for the rotation of students through centers and a way to keep track of centers.

- Provide an opportunity for students to select centers.

- Develop a signal or a problem-solving technique for students to use while they are at centers and you are working with other students.

- Periodically review what's working and not working at centers.

Managing and Organizing Literacy Centers

There are a variety of ways to organize and manage centers. Some teachers have students select literacy centers, while others choose the centers for the students to ensure they regularly rotate through them. No matter which approach you take, it is important to have a record-keeping system in place to monitor student participation in various centers.

Alternatives to Centers

Instead of centers, some teachers prefer to involve students in productive reading and writing work at their tables or desks. For Kindergarten and Grade 1, remember that children will need a chance to stretch and move periodically.

For students in Grades 3 and above, you will want to phase out most work at centers. For independent work, students can:

- Read silently a book of their choice at their independent level

- Write or draw in response to reading

- Engage in longer projects that involve research, reading, and writing.

GROUPING
STUDENTS

Your job is to take each student from his or her present level to a more advanced one. Therefore, there must be assessment of individual students. With class sizes ranging from 20 to 35, grouping for instruction makes sense. As teachers, we want to make learning manageable, while avoiding any negative aspects of grouping.

Fundamentals of Grouping

Assessment of Students' Knowledge Base

Students' knowledge base is the key element in selecting texts and planning instruction for groups so that they can read with 90 percent accuracy and use the skills that assure understanding. Other aspects to consider when selecting the best level for a group include:

- how well developing readers can control a strategy, such as analyzing a new word.
- the kinds of language students find understandable and which they find challenging.
- what concepts they know or what concepts they don't understand.
- the kinds of texts and genres they have experienced. For example, if they have handled only narrative texts, then informational texts may be difficult.

See pages 80–105 for help in assessing which level is best for a group.

Dynamic Grouping

Because students' individual needs change so often, ongoing observation of behavior and assessment of their knowledge and experience are essential to the guided reading process. Students progress at different rates, so regrouping is also ongoing. By grouping in different ways for different purposes, you can avoid labeling students with group names that are symbols of a static achievement level.

As you informally assess students' reading on a daily basis, you may wish to use the descriptions of **Behaviors to Notice and Support** on pages 80–105 for the level of book you are using. A quick, informal observation of students' reading will help you determine if the book was at the appropriate level.

- **Was this book too hard for this student? If the student can't read it independently with 85–95 percent accuracy and isn't using strategies as he or she reads, then the book is too hard.**
- **If the student reads with such fluency that there is no need for problem-solving behaviors, then the student should be reading a higher-level text for guided reading. Of course, the lower-level text will be useful for fluency practice.**

RUNNING
GUIDED READING GROUPS

Step 1   Select a Book

With students' needs in mind, select a book for a group of two to six. Use the **Characteristics of Text** to determine general level appropriateness and the description of **Behaviors to Notice and Support** to determine if students' reading ability matches that level. (See pages 80–105)

Depending on available time, each group of readers at levels A–J might read fewer books but must sustain attention and memory over several days or a week of reading. For readers in grades 3–6, the goal of independent and guided reading instruction is to enable students to read one chapter book a week or several shorter selections. No two groups will read exactly the same sequence of books, and groups will change as the assessment system helps track progress.

Step 2   Introduce the Book

Introducing the story is probably the most important and most difficult part of guided reading, and it is your opportunity to provide most of the support to the reader. A brief introduction helps a group to read successfully with minimal teacher support. You may tailor the introduction based on the group and the particular text. Depending on the level of difficulty and students' reading abilities, the introduction includes any combination of these elements:

- **a short conversation about the main idea of the text.**
- **a briefing on the author's purpose for writing and some important features of the plot or informational text.**
- **a description of the main characters, facts, or ideas in the book.**
- **a presentation of any unusual or unique language, such as a repetitive refrain or content words.**
- **a discussion of the concepts needed for an understanding of the text by activating prior knowledge.**
- **drawing attention to any aspects of print that you consider important such as captions, headings, charts and/or tables.**
- **instructions on how much to read and what to do when finished.**

Without actually reading the text to students, frame it in a meaningful way. Using oral language in a way that familiarizes students with some words they will meet in print helps prepare them to read. It isn't necessary to introduce every page, preteach words, or give a purpose for reading. The idea is to help students to be able to move through the text on their own. Any brief intervention should not interfere with the momentum of independent reading.

Step 3 Read the Book

Once the book has been introduced, students are ready to read. Unlike round-robin reading, in which each student reads a page or sentence, each student using guided reading reads the entire text.

• **Each student reads independently and problem-solves on his or her own.**

• **Reading may be oral or silent, depending on level and skill.**

As students read, you are nearby to observe them, providing support when necessary. As they read, note reading behaviors and offer praise when students use a strategy successfully. Students reading in levels A through J will be reading in a soft whisper. More advanced students will be reading silently. You can sample their oral reading by asking them to lift their voices to an audible level for a page or two. All students continue reading silently at their own rates as you sample oral reading from several of them.

If students have been placed in the appropriate level, they will problem-solve independently. However, if the whole group seems stuck, you may want to stop the group to assist in problem solving. You might also make teaching points, such as pointing out inflectional endings or consonant digraphs. Detours should be brief, not interrupting the momentum of students' reading.

Try to choose one student in the group daily to observe and interact with, helping him or her develop reading strategies, and encouraging the independent use of those strategies.

Step 4 Respond to the Book and Learn about Reading

After students read, first invite them to discuss the meaning of the text. Then select one or two teaching points to bring to their attention. What you select to teach depends on students' needs. You might focus on the meaning of a portion of text, on character interpretation, on information or facts, or on some aspect of word solving, such as multisyllabic words. For example, you might:

- promote fluency and phrasing by asking students to read aloud a favorite part of the story.
- help students focus on key ideas and language by having them find a turning point in the story, an informational part, or a description.
- help students figure out new, longer words by having them focus on word parts or known words.
- engage students in actively exploring how words work—building words, changing words, and noticing their features.
- help students interpret information provided in nonfiction features such as maps, charts, graphs, etc.

By following up the reading of a text in this way, you are helping students develop strategies that they can apply to the reading of other books. You are helping them learn the "how to" of reading and to move forward toward the goal of developing a reading process.

Step 5 Assess Behavior

The day after a new text is read, record the ability level of one child and note any progress. The **Behaviors to Notice and Support** can help you assess.

GUIDED READING AND THE
STRUGGLING READER

Guided reading groups shift as students' reading abilities and interests change. As you work with your guided reading groups, you will be able to identify students who need extra help. Guided reading provides many advantages in helping these students. After assessing their reading levels and pinpointing what skills and strategies they need help with, you can move struggling readers to groups that provide support. Within these groups, struggling readers will be able to read more with greater accuracy and fluency, as they will be working with text at their level. You will also be able to work with them on word skills that other students may already know.

Select books that match your students' reading levels.	Any group of struggling readers will likely vary widely in their abilities. Because of this, you will need to be careful in selecting texts that are interesting, yet not too difficult. Struggling readers are usually slow readers because they have been trying to read texts that are too challenging. Slow reading interferes with comprehension, but with appropriate texts, students will be able to increase their speed and improve their comprehension. Gradually, students should be able to take on more challenging texts as their reading abilities and confidence improve.
Involve students in reading every day.	Struggling readers need to spend more time actually reading than doing activities related to reading. Plan daily guided reading time for these students to increase the amount of time they read with support.
Plan additional time to introduce and discuss texts.	Extra time may be needed for introductions and discussions before and after reading to guide students in anticipating what they will read and then thinking about and understanding the text. This extra time will help students learn how to approach text as they prepare to read. It will also give them opportunities to discuss what they have learned and to hear others' ideas. Encourage students to ask questions, and teach them how to find answers in the text.
Include working with words in guided reading lessons.	At the end of each guided reading lesson, spend a few minutes showing students the principles of how words work. Have them apply the principles to selected examples. To make this work more interesting, create word games.
Allow time for silent reading.	As students' reading abilities improve, give them time to read silently as well as orally. Silent reading is beneficial in that it is faster than oral reading and text is easier to comprehend.

USING RESPONSE TO INTERVENTION

One tool educators can use to identify and help struggling readers is the Response to Intervention (RTI) framework. Many states have used RTI to identify students with specific learning disabilities as part of the Individuals with Disabilities Education Improvement Act (IDEA), implemented in 2004.

RTI provides for frequent, short tests to indicate a student's skill level relative to other students or established benchmarks. These short tests can be used to determine the success or failure of interventions and to determine how much additional support and instruction will be needed. The advantage of using RTI is that students who are at risk of having reading difficulties are identified early. Early identification can prevent some students from being placed in special education when all they need is a short period of intense intervention. With RTI, student progress is carefully monitored so that the intervention can be adjusted as needed. If students continue to have difficulty, then special education may be considered.

Implementing and using RTI requires a commitment on the part of teachers and administrators and may result in restructuring daily schedules and tasks. In practice, RTI can look very different from school to school, as it is tailored to fit specific situations and students. However, RTI programs do have common elements:

- **Instruction is based on individual students' needs.**
- **The program is preventive and proactive.**
- **All students are assessed.**
- **Assessments used must be reliable and valid.**
- **Response to assessment results is rapid and efficient.**
- **At-risk students are provided with various levels of intense intervention.**
- **Student progress is closely monitored.**
- **Professional development is a critical part of the program.**
- **Strong administrative support ensures commitment and resources.**

PROMPTS TO SUPPORT
PROBLEM-SOLVING STRATEGIES

adapted from *Guided Reading: Good First Teaching for All Children* (Fountas and Pinnell, 1996)

Throughout a guided reading session, the teacher prompts, encourages and confirms students' attempts at problem solving. The teacher helps students apply the in-the-head strategies they already know to new text. The teacher also helps students use a variety of strategies as they read. The key is to prompt with just the right amount of support so that eventually, each student will take over the strategizing for herself.

Prompts to Support Early Readers

• Read it with your finger.

• Try _____. Would that make sense?/Would that sound right?

• Do you think it looks like _____?

• Can you find _____? (a known or new word)

• Did you have enough (or too many) words?

• Read that again and start the word.

• Did it match?

• Did you run out of words?

Prompts to Support a Reader's Self-Monitoring Strategies

• Were you right?

• Why did you stop?

• What letter would you expect to see at the beginning? At the end?

• Would _____ fit there?/make sense?

• Check it. Does it look and sound right to you?

• What did you notice? (after hesitation or stop)

• Could it be _____?

• It could be _____, but look at _____.

• You almost got that. See if you can find what is wrong.

Prompts to Support a Reader's Use of All Sources of Information

- Check the picture.
- Does that sound right?
- You said (_____). Does that make sense?
- What's wrong with this? (Repeat what the student said.)
- Try that again and think what would make sense.
- What could you try?
- What can you do to help yourself?
- Try that again and think what would sound right.
- Do you know a word like that?

Prompts to Support a Reader's Self-Correction

- Something wasn't quite right.
- I like the way you worked that out.
- You're nearly right. Try that again.

Prompts to Support Phrased, Fluent Reading

- Can you read this quickly?
- Put your words together so it sounds like talking.

THE IMPORTANCE OF READING A
VARIETY OF TEXTS AND GENRES

Creating motivated readers is a challenge for any teacher faced with a class that varies widely in backgrounds, interests, and abilities. For students to become active readers, they must be exposed to a number and variety of texts and genres that are interesting and engaging, informative, accessible, representative of our diverse world, and include content appropriate for each student's age and gender. By selecting and introducing a variety of texts and genres over a period of time and demonstrating the many ways one can experience texts, you can help your students build a flexible reading process that will make any text accessible.

How do texts vary?

When students are exposed to a variety of good-quality texts within many genres, they can compare and connect texts across genres and become familiar with text characteristics. However, variety is more than an assortment of books of different genres. It includes format, special types of text across genres, different media, and a wide range of content and diversity.

Why is format important?

The sizes, shapes, designs, layouts, illustrations, binding, and placement and styles of print constitute some of the different formats in which text is presented. The types of formats students are most likely to encounter include fiction and nonfiction picture books, leveled readers, short stories, chapter books, series books, poems, short stories, short informational texts, magazines targeted to young readers, graphic novels, and comic books. Having available texts in different formats will increase opportunities for all students to find something they want to read. By experiencing texts in a wide range of formats, students also develop the ability to process different kinds of language and visual information.

How do genres vary?

Genre means types of text that are basically prose or poetry. Poetry comes in many forms, including traditional songs and rhymes, free verse, chants, and haiku. Prose can be divided into fiction and nonfiction, which is further divided into many types of text. Fiction can include realistic fiction, historical fiction, fantasy, science fiction, and traditional literature such as fables, folktales, and myths. Nonfiction includes biography; autobiography; memoirs; and informational, narrative, expository, and persuasive texts. Across genres, students will encounter text types with common features, including mysteries and stories of adventure, sports, and survival.

Why is genre important?

Different genres make different demands on readers. Students who are exposed to a wide variety of genres develop analytical-thinking skills and become more flexible in processing text. As their knowledge of genre grows, readers learn what to expect when they begin to read a text and can adjust their reading strategies accordingly. Even more important, they learn how to think within, beyond, and about their reading.

Through prose, students learn how language can be used to explain, describe, persuade, and elaborate. They become a part of the wider world, past and present, in nonfiction and enter imaginary worlds in fiction. They also discover how to think critically about what they read.

Why is diversity important?

Students also should be exposed to texts in both leveled books and books available for independent reading that reflect different cultures, languages, races, geographic regions, religions, and traditions. Through fiction and nonfiction texts that reflect our world, students will identify with characters in books and will learn about diversity, also learning to value it. In addition, they will discover viewpoints and perspectives that are different from their own.

How do different types of media help readers?

Providing variety in types of text is important in stretching students' thinking, but doing so also requires accessibility. Reading aloud varied texts gives all students quick and easy access to a wider range of genres and text levels they might not be ready to read independently. This same access can be provided with audiotapes or CDs and DVD movies based on books or stories. By making texts accessible to all students, you will have a basis for discussion that can involve the whole class.

Creating a Collection

When creating a classroom collection of books that will develop strong readers and writers and demand growth, remember to look for:

- **high-quality texts**
- **a variety of genres in fiction, nonfiction, and poetry**
- **favorite authors and illustrators**
- **enough copies for students' needs and your curriculum**
- **variety to interest students, both male and female**
- **variety in a range of reading levels**

GENRE DESCRIPTIONS AND KEY FEATURES

The *Scholastic Guided Reading Program: Fiction Focus 2nd Edition* provides a wide variety of genres, including fictional prose, poetry, graphic novels, and some nonfiction text.

FICTION

Poetry

Poetry is difficult to describe because it is a personal and emotional expression of the poet. Poetry's language can create an image in a few words and give readers an unexpected and fresh way to see something.

Key Features

- may have rhythms and patterns of language that are best discovered when read aloud
- may include rhyme within or at the end of lines
- may be free verse, which breaks from fixed stanzas and rhyme, instead setting up a rhythm through the language of the whole poem
- often breaks from conventional capitalization and punctuation

Realistic Fiction

Realistic fiction tells a story that could possibly happen to real people. The characters appear to have problems and goals that real people have, and attempt to solve these problems or reach goals with plausible actions. Readers often experience realistic fiction as truthful and can identify with and see themselves in the characters.

Key Features

- believable characters with human problems and desires
- setting that reflects real places and time
- character-driven events
- reasonable outcomes that reflect real life
- humor may be an element

Historical Fiction

Realistic fiction that takes place in the past is considered historical fiction. The story combines imagination and fact with characters as part of a fictional plot placed in a real historical setting. The setting is often integral to the plot as it affects how characters live and act as well as the events they are a part of.

Key Features

- believable characters
- setting that reflects a historical time and place
- details of how people live and work fit the time and place
- real historical people may appear as characters although what they do and say may be fictional unless historically documented

Fantasy

Fantasy includes stories that are not possible in real life. Characters or settings may be imaginary, or the events and characters' actions or abilities are not realistic. Once readers willingly accept the fantasy, the characters may be plausible with realistic problems, and the outcome may be reasonable.

Key Features	• characters may be imaginary, have magical abilities, and/or include personified animals
	• settings may be imaginary and change as characters travel through time or move into alternate worlds
	• plot may involve a conflict between good and evil

| **Science Fiction** | Science fiction is a type of fantasy that tells about events that have not happened yet or that could not happen in real life as it is known today. The imaginary elements are technology-driven instead of magical. The science established in a science fiction story may not be explained, but it must remain consistent to be believable. |

Key Features	• stories may take place in outer space, on other worlds, or in alternate dimensions
	• science and technology are used to create a world or characters that are not possible in present real life
	• the setting is usually important to the story as it affects characters and their actions

| **Traditional Literature** | Traditional literature encompasses stories that have been passed down orally through many generations. Different versions of the same tale often appear in many cultures. Readers expect recurring themes and structures, such as three wishes, journeys or quests, tricksters, or heroes who are often young. |

Key Features	• **Folktale:** an often humorous story that comes from a particular culture and is told orally until it is eventually recorded; includes stock characters that fill one function, simple conflicts and goals, fast action, repetitive events often in threes, and a definitive outcome
	• **Fable:** a brief story, usually with animal characters, that teaches a moral or a lesson that is stated clearly at the end of the story
	• **Fairy Tale:** a short story with magical characters and events; characters are usually all good or all bad; repetition in characters and actions; often begins with "once upon a time" and ends with "and they lived happily ever after"; has a more elaborate structure than a folktale
	• **Myth:** a story that explains something in nature; found in many cultures; often includes ancient gods who interact with humans; characters may also be personifications of natural forces such as the wind
	• **Legend:** a story that tells about the great deeds of a hero who may have been a real person in history, such as Davy Crockett; often mixed with mythical elements; may once have been based on fact, but is fictional in detail
	• **Trickster Tale:** a particular type of folktale in which a character, usually an animal, attempts to trick other characters into doing or giving something that will benefit the trickster; common tricksters include Anansi the Spider

Mystery	A mystery is a special type of fiction that centers on a problem that needs to be solved. The problem can be missing or stolen objects, puzzles, criminals to be identified and caught, and strange behavior that needs to be explained. Suspense and sometimes danger and fear play an important part in the action.
Key Features	• characters involved in solving a problem such as a puzzle or a crime • setting may be mysterious or ordinary • plot carries the story as characters follow clues to solve the mystery • mood is suspenseful • familiar forms are detective stories, strange adventures, and tales of espionage and crime
Play	A play is a story that is intended to be performed. Plays are character-driven, as they are told through what the characters say and do.
Key Features	• written in dialogue form with character names identifying the speaker • includes character actions and expressions briefly indicated, usually parenthetically • may include one or more acts with a clearly identified setting • usually includes in the beginning a list of characters and their characteristics such as name, age, and identity or profession
Novel	A novel is a longer work of fiction that contains all story elements, including characters, setting, plot, and theme. Because of its longer length, a novel can more fully develop characters over time and place. The length of a novel requires readers to develop reading stamina and the ability to follow plots and characters over an extended period of time and several reading sessions.
Key Features	• story is usually divided into chapters • may include several major and minor characters that are fully developed • may include story background in the beginning or as the story unfolds • may include several subplots • plot may include many events as action rises and falls • may include a resolution and events after the climax or turning point
Graphic Novel	Graphic novels are similar to comic books, but they tell a more complete story with a beginning, middle, and end. A graphic novel often resembles a novel in length and narrative. The term *graphic* refers to the pictorial nature of the novel.
Key Features	• story told through pictures • dialogue included in speech balloons • narrative may be within story frames or at the top of a page • characters developed through dialogue and illustration

NONFICTION

Informational Text	Informational text provides factual information. Content may be scientific or social, exploring the natural and physical world or people and places in the past or present. Informational text can be presented in a variety of formats including reference books, books on specific subjects or processes, magazines, CDs, or filmed documentaries.
Key Features	• provides information on a whole class of things, places, or people • describes and explains • compares and contrasts • includes technical vocabulary • often includes headings and subheadings to divide text • presents information through graphics such as photographs, charts, diagrams, and maps as well as text • includes labels and captions • includes a table of contents and an index • may include a bibliography
Narrative	Narrative nonfiction tells the story of an event or series of events that occur in the present or past. Background to the event is often provided along with specific details about what happened and who was involved.
Key Features	• describes an event or series of events, including dates, time, places, and the people involved • may include graphics such as photographs, illustrations, and charts • may include a table of contents, an index, and a bibliography
Biography/Autobiography	A biography or an autobiography is about a single historical or current person. It may cover the person's whole life or a significant period. An autobiography is written by the person who is the subject of the story. An autobiography may take the form of a memoir in which the person relates his or her experiences during a meaningful time. A biography is written by an author about a person who is the subject of the book.
Key Features	• covers one person's life or a significant period of that person's life • usually written about an important person • may include photographs and illustrations • may include a table of contents, an index, and/or a bibliography

INCLUDING **NONFICTION AND INFORMATIONAL TEXT** IN PRIMARY CLASSROOMS

adapted from *Reading & Writing Informational Text in the Primary Grades*
(Duke and Bennett-Armistead, 2003)

Guided Reading: Fiction Focus, 2nd Edition includes a variety of nonfiction and informational texts as part of its genre array. Often the terms "informational text" and "nonfiction" are used interchangeably, but they are not the same. Informational text is a type of nonfiction—a very important type. Nonfiction includes any text that is factual. (Or, by some definitions, any type of literature that is factual, which would exclude text such as menus and street signs.) Informational text differs from other types of nonfiction in that its primary purpose is to convey information about the natural or social world, and typically includes particular linguistic features such as headings and technical vocabulary.

It is important to note that within informational text, there are several different types of text that might be considered informational text genres or subgenres including:

- **reference books such as encyclopedias, field guides, and so on**
- **"all about" books, on topics such as spiders or dinosaurs**
- **process-informational books including books about how an animal develops from conception to adulthood or about how some substance is created or transformed**
- **magazines, newspapers, posters, pamphlets, Web sites, CD-ROMs, and so on**

Why focus on informational and nonfiction texts in primary classrooms? There are a number of arguments for doing so. Some of these arguments have a more solid research base than others, and some may be more compelling than others. But the research available to this point is clear. Students need to encounter more informational text because:

Informational Text Is Key to Success in Later Schooling
We have all heard that from around fourth grade on, "reading to learn" is a major focus in school (Chall, 1983). Students encounter more textbooks and other forms of informational text as they move through the grades. The tests they take contain increasingly more difficult informational texts. If teachers include more informational text in early schooling, they put students in a better position to handle the reading and writing demands of their later schooling.

Informational Text Is Ubiquitous in Society
Several studies have looked at the kinds of things people write *outside* of school—what students and adults read and write in their workplaces, homes, and communities. Again and again these studies have shown that adults read a great deal of nonfiction, including informational text (e.g., Venezky, 1982, Smith, 2000). This is not likely to change and, in fact, in our increasingly information-based economy, it may only increase. According to one study (Kamil & Lane, 1998), 96 percent of the text on the World Wide Web is expository.

Informational Text Is Preferred Reading Material for Many Students

When researchers investigate the kinds of texts students like to read, they've found that different students have different reading preferences. Some students seem to prefer informational text, some seem to prefer narrative text, and many don't seem to have preferences for any particular genre. For those students who prefer informational text—students Ron Jobe and Mary Dayton-Sakari (2002) call "Info-Kids"—including more informational text in classrooms may improve attitudes toward reading and even serve as a catalyst for overall literacy development (Caswell & Duke, 1998).

Informational Text Builds Knowledge of the Natural and Social World

By definition, informational text conveys information about the natural and social world (Duke, 2000). Reading and listening to informational text therefore can develop students' knowledge of that world (e.g., Anderson & Guthrie, 1999; Duke & Kays, 1998). This in turn can promote students' comprehension of subsequent texts they read (e.g., Wilson & Anderson, 1986), because it can build background knowledge.

Young Children Can Handle Informational Text

The research is clear. Young children *can* interact successfully with informational text. (See Dreher, 2000; Duke, 2003; and Duke, Bennett-Armistead, & Roberts, 2002, 2003, for reviews of research on this point.) Studies show that Kindergartners can develop knowledge of information-book language and content from information-book read alouds and shared readings. Primary-grade students can comprehend informational text that they read themselves. Research also indicates that young children can write informational text. So you needn't worry that informational text is inherently "over the heads" of your students, and you should be able to respond with confidence to colleagues who have doubts.

THINKING **WITHIN**, **BEYOND**, AND **ABOUT** THE TEXT

Adapted from *Teaching for Comprehending and Fluency: Thinking, Talking, and Writing About Reading, K-8* (Irene C. Fountas and Gay Su Pinnell, 2006)

When proficient readers process a text, they simultaneously draw on a wide range of strategic actions that are physical, emotional, cognitive, and linguistic. As students learn the skills and strategies they need to make sense of a text, this process becomes more effective and automatic. Eventually, the reading process becomes unconscious. In order to reach this point, students need to learn how proficient readers think about reading. Teachers may often interpret this as making sure students comprehend what they are reading. However, checking for comprehension by asking endless questions during reading can turn into an interrogation that interferes with the reading process. Having students learn and focus on one reading strategy at a time also can make the reading process less effective. Instead, students need guidance in how to integrate strategic actions and use them effectively with many kinds of texts. For the teacher, this means knowing what readers must be able to do and the information they need to access to process a text.

Readers access a wide range of information that is both visible and invisible. Visible information is what students see as words and art in the text. As they read, readers recognize letters, words, punctuation, format, and text structures, and they attach meaning to what they see. Proficient readers are barely aware of this processing of visual information as they focus on meaning. Invisible information—including the knowledge and experience of language, facts, and the world both past and present—is what readers know and think about as they respond to visual information. Such personal knowledge is different for each student and is shaped by family, culture, and community. As students learn about different cultures and communities, they expand their perspectives and make new connections. Many of the texts they encounter can become the basis for this expansion.

Another form of invisible information is readers' experiences with many kinds of text, including knowledge of genres, text structures, and formats. This knowledge helps readers form expectations and predictions about a new text, access meaning as they read, and respond to the text after reading.

Different kinds of texts make different demands on readers. Texts that students can read independently help them build their knowledge. Texts that students can read with teacher support challenge them to develop new strategic actions for reading. You can help students meet these demands by giving them opportunities to think about their reading within, beyond, and about text.

Thinking Within the Text

When readers think within the text, they gather basic information from the text and determine its basic meaning. To do so, readers must process the text by:

- decoding words and using word meaning and what they know about language
- searching for information, and noting and sorting important details
- determining how the text is organized
- monitoring themselves for accuracy and understanding
- adjusting reading speed and technique according to the type of text
- sustaining fluency

Understanding the basic meaning of a text forms the foundation for higher thinking skills. By thinking within the text, readers can gather important information and summarize what they have read.

Thinking Beyond the Text

When readers think beyond the text, they go more deeply into its meaning beyond their literal understanding of it. They are able to:

- make predictions
- connect their reading to their own experiences
- relate the text to similar texts
- integrate what they know with new information
- infer ideas that are not directly stated
- think about the greater meaning of the text

Thinking beyond the text allows readers to understand character motivations, explore how setting influences the story, and follow more complex plots. They also identify and learn new information that they can incorporate into what they already know and understand.

Thinking About the Text

To think about the text, readers analyze and critique what they read. They examine a text to:

- note how it is constructed
- note how the writer uses language
- identify literary devices
- determine how the writer has provided information, such as using compare and contrast, description, or cause and effect
- identify characteristics of the genre
- use their own knowledge to think critically about ideas
- evaluate quality and authenticity

Thinking about the text helps readers move beyond identifying likes and dislikes and helps them learn more about how texts work. It also helps them better appreciate different genres, good-quality writing, and their own writing.

Guiding Students to Think Within, Beyond, and About the Text

Thinking about the text is a complex process that is difficult to teach or demonstrate. Although there is value in directing readers to important aspects of the text, effective reading strategies should be shown as working together in an integrated process. You can talk about the text before reading, at certain points during reading, and after reading to motivate questions and ideas. You can share your own ideas and demonstrate the different kinds of thinking readers do. However, instruction must still allow readers to respond to the text in a way that expands and expresses their own thinking.

In your guided reading groups, you can help your students learn how to think within, beyond, and about the text by being mindful of:

- **the important aspects of processing related to reading the texts you have selected**
- **what you want your students to do**
- **the learning opportunities presented by a particular text**
- **how students might respond to text features that could open opportunities for teaching**

What follows are some tips about how to help students think within, beyond, and about fiction and nonfiction texts.

Fiction

To think within the text, help students to:

- **follow the events of the plot; show how to think about what happens first, then next**
- **gather information about characters and setting by giving examples of what to look for**
- **learn about the characters by noting how they are described, what they say or think, what others say about them, and how they change over the course of the story**
- **identify the conflict or problem, and the solution**
- **solve words by thinking about their meaning in context**

To think beyond the text, help students to:

- **infer character motivations and feelings by looking for evidence in the text and by making connections between themselves and the characters**
- **infer why characters change over time by looking for evidence in the story**
- **connect the text to background knowledge, personal experiences, and other texts by thinking about other stories the text reminds them of, what they already know about the topic, place, or time, and how the plot or characters are similar to another text**
- **predict how the problem is solved by thinking about what has happened, what will happen next, and what is known about the characters**
- **understand the theme or message by thinking about what the writer is trying to say**
- **relate the theme, plot, or characters to their own lives**
- **infer how events are significant**
- **note new ideas, identify how their thinking has changed and what they have learned**

To think about the text, help students to:

- evaluate the importance of the setting by thinking how the text would be different if set in another time or place, or how the story changed when the setting changed
- notice how the writer made the characters realistic
- pay attention to the plot structure by thinking about how the story is organized, how the writer shows the passing of time, and identifying any flashbacks
- note aspects of the writer's craft by looking for language that helped them clarify something
- evaluate the quality or authenticity of the text

Nonfiction

To think within the text, help students to:

- gather and remember important information by deciding what they will learn from the text and what they think is important
- gather and remember information from the illustrations and graphics
- use different tools, such as a table of contents, headings, captions, index, and glossary, to locate and use information

To think beyond the text, help students to:

- identify new information and add it to their existing knowledge by thinking how their ideas might have changed after reading the text
- make connections between the text and background knowledge, personal experience, and other texts by thinking what the text reminds them of and what they already knew about the topic
- infer cause and effect by thinking about what happened and why
- identify the problem and the solution posed by the writer
- notice and understand the sequence of events
- analyze description by examining details and looking for examples in the text

To think about the text, help students to:

- recognize if and how the writer uses cause and effect, problem and solution, description, sequence, and compare and contrast by noticing how the writer constructed the story
- evaluate the authenticity and accuracy of the text by thinking about why the text seems accurate and how facts could be checked
- decide how the writer made the topic interesting by looking for specific examples
- analyze why the writer chose particular information to include in graphics

THE IMPORTANCE OF TALKING ABOUT BOOKS

Discussing books should be a rich part of every student's reading life. When students are encouraged and given opportunities to talk about books with peers and their teachers, they become motivated to share what they liked best about a text—and what they found interesting or surprising. They learn how to ask questions to find out what other students thought about a text and how to recommend a favorite book. They experience having their opinions valued rather than evaluated. They also discover that talking about books is fun.

Getting students to talk about books beyond the usual "I liked it" or "I didn't like it" or short answers to questions about specific texts is often difficult. However, there are a variety of ways you can spark discussion about books in your classroom including book clubs, literature circles, and topic discussions.

Interactive Read-Aloud

Before students can effectively discuss books with others, they need to learn how to talk about books. You can help them learn by conducting interactive read-alouds in which you demonstrate how to talk about books. Begin by selecting a text you know your students will enjoy, or invite them to select a text from several you offer. After you introduce the text, read it aloud and pause occasionally to demonstrate how to talk about the book. Then invite students to join in. Students can share comments or questions or respond to a discussion prompt with the whole group, another student, or a small group. After reading, you can invite students to comment on what the text means, link it to other books, reflect on the writer's craft, and evaluate text quality.

During an interactive read-aloud, students learn how to:

- **focus on the text**
- **use suitable words when talking about a text**
- **listen actively and respect others' ideas**
- **build on others' comments**
- **back up their opinions with evidence from the text**

Through active participation, students learn that they are expected to respond to one another's comments and that everyone should participate.

Literature Discussion Groups

Once students have learned how to talk about books, they can try out their skills in literature discussion groups. These small groups, each consisting of four to six students, operate under many different names including book clubs, literature circles, and topic discussions. They all are organized around students sharing their thinking about texts.

In literature discussion groups, students are in charge of their own thinking, talking, and writing. They have a chance to share what they think within, beyond, and about a text. As a result, interest in their own learning grows.

At first, you will need to be closely involved with book clubs and literature circles to set routines and select books. Choose books that are developmentally appropriate as well as interesting. Have a copy for each student in a group. Be sure that everyone in the class is a part of a discussion group. A group can consist of students who are interested in a particular author, topic, or genre. Some groups might be all girls or all boys.

Designate where and when book clubs will meet. Encourage members to come prepared by having read the selected book and spending some time thinking about it, deciding on information and ideas to share. Have students sit in a circle at a table or on the floor so they can see one another. You may want to post a list of text elements for fiction and nonfiction for the group to refer to as they discuss the book. Book club meetings will normally last about fifteen minutes for younger students and up to thirty minutes for older, more experienced students.

You can participate by helping groups get their discussions started, move beyond a sticking point, or continue when they think they have run out of things to say. Note how group members work with each other, and be sure they give evidence for their opinions from the text or personal experience. Encourage them to ask questions, especially when they don't understand something. As students become more experienced in discussing books, you can move gradually into the role of observer, interacting with groups only as needed.

As you observe book discussions, pay attention to both process and content. Some groups may be proficient at the process of talking about a book but not about the content, so they end up saying little about the deeper meaning of a book. The purpose of a book club is for students to learn how to explore the meaning of a text and express their thinking about that text. Other groups may have many ideas to share, but they don't know how to organize their meeting. You may need to spend some time with these groups to remind them how to lead a discussion, let everyone have a turn, listen when others are speaking, and participate in the discussion.

USING THE TEACHING CARDS

Each card provides teachers with a quick and essential analysis of the book students will read.

Tangerine

Summary & Standard
Paul Fisher sees more than his thick glasses would allow and tells his diary all that happens when his family moves from Houston to small-town Florida. Students will read to better understand the various cultures of the United States.

Author: Edward Bloor
Genre: Realistic Fiction

Word Count: 250+
Theme/Idea: facing challenges

Meets standards and makes real-world connections.

Making Connections: Text to Self
Students may have prior knowledge about moving to a new home or new town or attending a new school. Discuss what students experienced when making these changes.

Extend the real-world connection by talking about how students would want to be treated at a new school. Ask for suggestions as to how best to welcome a new student. Discuss practical difficulties a student might encounter at a new school during his or her first week.

For additional teaching ideas and resources, see http://www2.scholastic.com/browse/collateral.jsp?id=972.

Builds rich oral and written vocabulary.

Vocabulary
Essential Words: development, eclipse, handicap, majority, minority, portable, regulation, threatening

Related Words for Discussion: admiration, fame, perceive, reputation

Genre
Realistic Fiction Remind students that realistic fiction has characters, settings, and conflicts that may be found in real life.

Supportive Book Features
Text The text is organized as a diary with dated entries. Its strict chronology and first-person narrative create structural simplicity.

Content Students will be familiar with the difficulties and challenges that can arise when trying to fit in with new friends, a new school, or even new siblings or other family members.

Praise students for specific use of "Behaviors to Notice and Support" on page 100 of the *Guided Reading Teacher's Guide*.

Challenging Book Features
Text The book has nearly 300 pages and a great deal of text on each page. Remind students that the dates at the beginning of the diary entry can help them follow the sequence of events in the story.

Vocabulary Students may not be familiar with idioms, colloquialisms, and figurative language used in the book. Read aloud sections where these expressions are used and explain that they make the text more lively and often give it added meaning. Also, these devices give dialogue the quality of natural speech.

Level U

ELL Bridge
To help students understand the organization of the book, talk about keeping a journal. Explain that journal entries are dated and arranged chronologically. A journal can be used to record daily personal experiences in the order in which they happen. Have students keep a log of how they spend one day, complete with the time each event or activity happened. Then have them compare their logs to the diary entries in the book, discussing how the dates/times help the reader understand the sequence of events.

■ SCHOLASTIC

Easily adapts lessons to meet the needs of English language learners.

Teaching Options

Developing Comprehension

Thinking Within the Text
Have students discuss what they learned about Paul. How was he able to cope with the change in schools? Summarize the events that Paul experienced and how he handled each situation.

Thinking Beyond the Text
Ask students to describe Lake Windsor Middle School and Tangerine Middle School. Have students make connections by asking which school is more similar to theirs and why. Have students predict how Paul might have felt if he had transferred to their school. Would he have been just as excited? What if Erik had transferred to their school?

Thinking About the Text
Remind students that figurative language refers to language that means something beyond the dictionary definition of the words. Point to the line *If you think we're slugs . . .* on page 45. Ask: *Is Paul saying that the students are actually slugs? Why does he make this comparison?* Have students notice and point to other examples of how the writer uses figurative language to describe actions, characters, and how people feel.

Compare and Contrast
Remind students that authors often compare and contrast things and people to show how they are alike and different. Point out how the book contrasts Paul's two schools. Have students identify ways in which the schools and the students at each are different.

- Ask: *How does Paul feel about these differences throughout the book? Are there any similarities between the schools?*

- Have students support their answers with sentences or passages from the story.

For more prompts and ideas for teaching problem-solving strategies, see page 22 of the *Guided Reading Teacher's Guide*.

Developing Phonics and Word-Solving Strategies

Varying Words With Prefixes and Suffixes
Explain that prefixes, suffixes, or both can be added to base words to form new words.

- Ask students to identify the base word that can be found in both *undeveloped* and *development* (*develop*). Then have them identify the affixes that have been added (*un-*, *-ment*). Challenge students to use these words in a sentence. Then have students list other prefixes and suffixes.

- Ask them to add prefixes and suffixes to *pack* to form variations of the word.

Developing Fluency
Model expressive reading of a passage from the book, stressing appropriate pauses. Have students read the passage aloud, paying attention to phrasing and using appropriate expression.

Oral Language/Conversation
Talk About Reputation Lead a discussion about reputation. Have a volunteer look up *reputation* in the dictionary and read the definition aloud. Talk about how a person's reputation may or may not describe his or her character. Discuss Erik's reputation and how people perceived him.

Extending Meaning Through Writing

- Challenge students to write a diary entry from the point of view of another character in the book, such as Theresa, who shows Paul around the school. **(Narrative)**

- Have students write a page explaining why the sinkhole, termites, and muck fires are metaphors for Paul's life. **(Expository)**

Other Books
Report to the Principal's Office by Jerry Spinelli
The Secret Garden by Frances Hodgson Burnett

ASSESSMENT
OBSERVATION

Overview

We define assessment as the collection of information about a student's learning, and evaluation as the judgment about the student's strengths and specific needs based on this information. Assessment should be continuous—based on observation and informal measures of reading performance. Evaluation should provide a guide for teaching decisions that will help the student's learning.

To assess and evaluate a student's literacy development, information needs to be collected to demonstrate the following:

- **how a student uses and responds to oral language in various settings.**
- **what a student knows about reading and writing.**
- **how a student uses reading and writing in various settings.**
- **how a student values reading and writing.**

The Guided Reading Program is structured to give information on different kinds of literacy skills for students with varied learning needs. The program supports literacy development in reading, writing, listening, and speaking. These literacy activities provide a wealth of assessment information.

Purposes of Assessment

As a student progresses from a beginning reader and writer to a fluent reader and writer, assessment may have several purposes:

- **to establish what a student initially knows about literacy.**
- **to identify a student's instructional reading level.**
- **to monitor a student's pattern of strengths.**
- **to establish a student's facility with informational text.**

Assessment needs to take place at the beginning of the school year to know what foundational skills students have and to identify potential skill needs. All school-age students know something about oral and written language and are ready to learn more. Some may have knowledge about environmental print but little experience with books or with writing. Others may be confident with books and with some writing.

Observation

One of the best ways to assess an individual student's learning is through observation. For a well-rounded view of the student, try to observe him or her throughout the day in a variety of settings, such as during small-group and whole-class instruction, during independent reading time, or in the classroom library. What exactly can you observe?

Some suggestions include:

- **oral language ability**
- **interests**
- **attitudes**
- **book-handling behaviors**
- **choices during "free time"**
- **peer relationships**
- **specific behaviors related to print**

Ask yourself questions such as the following when observing a student's behaviors related to print:

- **When the student reads or works with print, does he or she approach the task confidently?**
- **Does the student have a strategy for attempting unfamiliar words in reading and writing?**
- **Does the student read and write for different purposes?**
- **Can the student retell what he or she reads in a logical order?**
- **Does the student select reading materials suited to his or her personal interests?**
- **Does the student select reading materials suited to his or her level of reading development?**

Answers to these kinds of questions will help you make instructional decisions and set goals for an individual student, and will help the student progress in learning.

Make your observations systematic rather than random. Decide whom to focus on. Select one student or several at a time to closely watch. Keep a record for each student, noting what you see by recording it on self-adhesive stickies or peel-off labels that can be attached to the student's personal folder. Alternatively, keep a class list for easy referral.

When behaviors are observed, a check (✓) may be used. You may also wish to make a slash (/) the first time the behavior is observed and convert the slash to an X when you feel the behavior is performed with frequency. Indicating dates is helpful.

Decide when to observe. Observe during a time students are normally using books, when they first come into the room in the morning, or during a time they are involved in various learning centers. You may need to initiate the experience with students who do not independently go to books. Collect pertinent data, including written work samples and recordings of oral reading, and keep anecdotal records. Speak with parents for additional input.

ASSESSMENT
RUNNING RECORDS

An effective reader uses the visual information, based on knowledge of language and the content, to predict what comes next in the text, to check this prediction by taking in new visual information or by thinking about whether the prediction makes sense, and to confirm or reject this prediction in the light of this new information. If the prediction is rejected, the reader self-corrects.

When a student reads aloud, you can record what is read and look more closely at what the student is thinking and doing. Oral reading miscues reveal a student's reading strategies. Any miscues can be analyzed to make teaching decisions about the suitability of the level of the guided reading books being read and about the type of help a student may need. One way of doing this is to take a running record of oral reading.

Using a Running Record
Follow this assessment procedure to periodically monitor reading strategies.

First Step	Select something that is known to the student for him or her to read orally. (If it is too familiar, the reading may not reveal much information about the child's thinking.) This may be: • **a guided reading book;** • **a poem;** • **a dictated piece of the student's writing;** • **some of the student's published personal writing.**
Second Step	Ask the student to read the selected piece aloud. Record the student's reading in one of these ways: • **Record the correct reading and miscues on a blank piece of paper as the student reads, keeping the same linear arrangement of the text.** OR • **Make a copy of the text and mark the miscues on it as the student reads.**
Third Step	Tabulate the miscues. Use symbols to indicate what the student is doing. Some usual conventions follow.

Accurate reading	✓✓✓	(checks follow test pattern)
Substitution	wet (*child*)	
	Went (*text*)	
Attempt	w-we-wet	
	went	
Self-correction	wet	
	Went SC	
Omission	-	(or circle word)
	went	
Insertion	is	(or use carat)
	went	
Teacher told	-	(or underline word)
	Went T	
Repetition (of word or sentence)	R2 (numeral indicated number of repeats)	(or wavy underlines)

Evaluation: Analysis of the Running Record

Miscues in oral reading performance help you to identify the strategies a student uses. Ask yourself why the student makes each error. To determine what cues the student depends on, consider the following:

- **Does the student use visual cues from letters and words, such as *they* for *them*?**

- **Does the student use context clues to construct meaning? Inaccurate reading that makes sense indicates the student is probably using prior knowledge or familiar oral language.**

- **Does the student use knowledge of the grammatical structure of language? Again, the student's own oral language may influence a response.**

Make your best guess as to what cues the student uses, recording by the miscues *v* for visual cues, *m* for meaning, and *s* for structure. One or more types of cues might be used for any miscue. By analyzing each miscue in this way you can get an indication of the strategies the student is using, as well as those not being used or those being overused. Also notice instances of self-correction. Self-correction is an important skill in good reading.

Finally, make any notes on the running record about behaviors during the session. All of this information will assist you in assessing the student.

Running Records as a Regular Monitoring Tool

For each student who is able to read some type of continuous text, it is useful to take a running record about every six weeks. Repeat more often for students for whom you have concerns. For fluent readers it would only be necessary at the beginning, middle, and end of the school year.

Establish a system. For example, you might choose one student per school day, keeping the dated record and analysis in each student's portfolio to monitor the progress during the year. Select a time when you can hear the student read without interruptions, such as when other students are engaged in individual quiet reading.

Sample Running Record

Name: _____ Date: _____

Title: _____

PAGE	TEXT INFORMATION USED	RUNNING RECORD	
4	The animals had a picnic	✓ ✓ have ✓ ✓	v, m
	To celebrate the fair.	✓ ✓ ✓ ✓	
	They all brought something tasty	✓ ✓ bought ✓ t/testy/SC	v, m, s
	For everyone to share.	✓ ✓ ✓ ✓	
7	The lambs brought yams.	✓ ✓ bought ✓	v, m, s
	The bees brought peas.	✓ ✓ bought ✓	v, m, s
	The poodles brought noodles	✓ ✓ bought ✓	v, m, s
	All sprinkled with cheese.	✓ sprin/sprinkle/SC ✓	
8	The cheetahs brought pitas.	✓ ✓ bought pasta/T	v, m, s
	The mice brought rice.	✓ ✓ bought ✓	v, m, s
	The moose brought juice	✓ ✓ bought ✓	v, m, s
	And a bucket of ice.	✓ ✓ ✓ ✓ ✓	
11	The pigs brought figs.	✓ ✓ bought ✓	v, m, s
	The bears brought pears.	✓ ✓ bought ✓	v, m, s
	The apes brought grapes	✓ ✓ bought ✓	v, m, s
	And some picnic chairs.	✓ ✓ ✓ ✓	
12	The raccoons brought spoons.	✓ ✓ ✓ ✓	
	The moles brought bowls.	✓ ✓ ✓ ✓	
	The storks brought forks	✓ ✓ ✓ fo/fork/SC	
	And some cinnamon rolls.	✓ ✓ c/cam/camon/T	v
15	The snakes brought cakes	✓ snake bought ✓	v, m, s
	And I brought the tea.	✓ ✓ ✓ ✓ ✓	
	It was a wild picnic –	✓ ✓ ✓ ✓ ✓	
	Just the animals and me!	✓ ✓ ✓ ✓ ✓	

v=visual, m=meaning, s=structure

Calculations

Note: In the example the student repeatedly misread the word *brought* as *bought*. There are two approaches to counting this error: as one error that is repeated or as multiple errors (which the student failed to self-correct).

- **Calculation of Accuracy Rate**

  If *bought* is counted as only one error, accuracy rate is calculated as follows:

  $$102 - (5/102 \times 100) = 95\%$$

  If *bought* is counted as an error each time it is misread, the accuracy rate is calculated as follows:

  $$102 - (15/102 \times 100) = 85\%$$

  The calculation of the accuracy rate is expressed by the following generic formula:

  $$T - (E/T \times 100) = AR$$

- **Calculation of Self-Correction Rate**

  If *bought* is counted as only one error, self-correction rate is $(5+3)/3 = 2.6$

  If *bought* is counted as an error each time it is misread, self-correction rate is $(15+3)/3 = 6$

  The calculation of the self-correction rate can be expressed by the following formula:

  $$(E + SC)/SC = SCR$$

T = total number of words	E = number of errors
AR = accuracy rate	SC = number of self-corrections
SCR = self-correction rate	

Teacher's Notes

Adib told the story (pointing to picture) and answered questions. Adib is using all strategies when reading and seems to have cross-checked one cue against another to self-correct. I could draw his attention to the difference between brought *and* bought. *This book is at a suitable level of difficulty for instruction.*

Note that space has also been provided for you to ask your own comprehension questions and record children's responses.

Evaluation of Suitability of Books

If a student is reading at an appropriate instructional level, approximately 94% of the text should be read accurately. An attempt at a word that is eventually correct is not an error; record this as a self-correction and tally it as accurately read. By calculating the percentage of accurately read words and analyzing the types of errors, you'll be able to determine whether the student is reading books at the appropriate instructional level, and you'll be able to choose the right guided reading books for individuals and groups.

Students may select a guided reading book to have it read to them or to read with a partner. In these instances the book may be easier or harder than the instructional level.

RUNNING RECORD
BENCHMARK BOOK LEVEL A

Running Record Sheet
Helping

Name _____ Date _____

24 Words   Level A   Accuracy Rate _____

PAGE	TEXT	RUNNING RECORD ANALYSIS
Page 3	I help my mom.	
Page 5	I help my dad.	
Page 7	I help my sister.	
Page 9	I help my cat.	
Page 11	I help my dog.	
Page 12	I like to help.	

Comprehension:

1) _____

_____

_____

_____

2) _____

_____

_____

_____

RUNNING RECORD
BENCHMARK BOOK LEVEL B

Running Record Sheet
Off to the City

Name _____   Date _____

43 Words   Level B   Accuracy Rate _____

PAGE	TEXT	RUNNING RECORD ANALYSIS
Page 2	Dad and Kim went off to the city.	
Page 3	They went past the pond.	
Page 4	They went past the red barn.	
Page 5	They went past the train station.	
Page 6	They went past the school.	
Page 7	Dad and Kim went to see Grandma.	
Page 8	Dad and Kim went back home.	

Comprehension:

1) _____

_____

_____

_____

2) _____

_____

_____

_____

RUNNING RECORD
BENCHMARK BOOK LEVEL C

Running Record Sheet
The Big Blue Sea

Name _____   Date _____

68 Words   Level C   Accuracy Rate _____

PAGE	TEXT	RUNNING RECORD ANALYSIS
Page 2	A little fish lives in the big blue sea.	
Page 4	A big turtle lives in the big blue sea.	
Page 6	A little sea star lives in the big blue sea.	
Page 8	A big jellyfish lives in the big blue sea.	
Page 10	A little sea horse lives in the big blue sea.	
Page 12	A big, big octopus lives in the big blue sea.	
Page 14	Big animals and little animals live in the big blue sea.	

Comprehension:

1) _____

_____

_____

_____

2) _____

_____

_____

_____

RUNNING RECORD
BENCHMARK BOOK LEVEL D

Running Record Sheet
The Little Red Hen

Name _____   Date _____

50 Words   Level D   Accuracy Rate _____

PAGE	TEXT	RUNNING RECORD ANALYSIS
Page 2	There was a little red hen. She found a grain of wheat. The little red hen said, "Who will plant this grain of wheat?"	
Page 3	"Not I," said the duck. "Not I," said the dog. "Not I," said the cat. "Then I will plant the wheat," said the little red hen.	

Comprehension:

1) _____

_____

_____

_____

2) _____

_____

_____

_____

RUNNING RECORD
BENCHMARK BOOK LEVEL E

Running Record Sheet
Fred's Wish for Fish

Name _____ Date _____

128 Words   Level E   Accuracy Rate _____

PAGE	TEXT	RUNNING RECORD ANALYSIS
Page 2	Fred and Dad went to the pet store. Dad said, "Look at the fish, Fred!" Fred said, "I wish I had some fish." Fred did not have any fish. Fred said, "Can we get some fish, please?" Dad said, "Okay!"	
Page 4	Kate from the pet store came to help. Fred said, "I want orange fish. I want black and white fish. I want fish with lots of colors!" Kate put the fish in a bag with water. Fred and Dad went home.	
Page 6	Fred looked at his fish. He had orange fish. He had black and white fish. He had fish with lots of colors. Fred was happy!	
Page 8	Dad said, "Now you have a lot of fish." Fred said, "Thank you, Dad! I love my fish! And I love **you**!"	

Comprehension:

1) _____

_____

_____

_____

2) _____

_____

_____

_____

RUNNING RECORD
BENCHMARK BOOK LEVEL F

Running Record Sheet
The Country Mouse and the Town Mouse

Name _____   Date _____

126 Words   Level F   Accuracy Rate _____

PAGE	TEXT	RUNNING RECORD ANALYSIS
Page 2	What did Country Mouse do? She called Town Mouse. She asked Town Mouse to dinner.	
Page 4	What did Country Mouse do? She put nuts and berries in a basket.	
Page 6	What did Country Mouse do? She met Town Mouse at the door.	
Page 8	What did Country Mouse do? She gave Town Mouse berries and nuts. "Do you like the dinner?" asked Country Mouse. "I do, but I have more to eat in town. Come for dinner! You will see," said Town Mouse.	
Page 10	What did Country Mouse do? She left her country home.	
Page 11	What did Country Mouse do? She went to town. She went to Town Mouse's home.	
Page 12	What did Country Mouse do? She saw a lot of food. "This is how a mouse eats in town!" said Town Mouse.	

Comprehension:

1) _____

_____

2) _____

_____

Running Record Sheet
Justin's New Bike

Name _____   Date _____

122 Words   Level G   Accuracy Rate _____

PAGE	TEXT	RUNNING RECORD ANALYSIS
Page 3	Danny and Justin went to the bike track. Justin had a new bike. Danny's bike was old.	
Page 4	They looked at the other kids riding up and down the hills on the track.	
Page 6	Justin looked at Danny going around the track.	
Page 7	"I can do that," said Danny. "Look at me!" he shouted.	
Page 8	Danny was going very fast! He made lots of dust.	
Page 9	Justin looked down at his new bike. He looked at Danny speeding around the bike track.	
Page 10	"I can go faster than you," shouted Justin.	
Page 11	Justin took off down the first hill. "Look out, Danny," shouted Justin. "Here I come!"	
Page 12	Justin went speeding around the track after Danny. Dust flew up from the track. The boys went flying over the little hills …	

Comprehension:

1) _____

_____

_____

2) _____

_____

_____

RUNNING RECORD
BENCHMARK BOOK LEVEL H

Running Record Sheet
Sammy the Seal

Name _____   Date _____

113 Words   Level H   Accuracy Rate _____

PAGE	TEXT	RUNNING RECORD ANALYSIS
Page 7	It was feeding time at the zoo. All the animals were getting their food.	
Page 8	The lions ate their meat.	
Page 9	The elephants ate their hay.	
Page 10	The monkeys ate their bananas.	
Page 11	The bears ate their honey.	
Page 12	Then it was time for the seals to be fed. Mr. Johnson took them fish.	
Page 13	"Hooray for fish!" said the seals. They jumped in the water.	
Page 14	Soon the basket was empty. "That is all there is," said Mr. Johnson. "There is no more."	
Page 15	"Thank you for the fish," said the seals. "They were good." The seals were happy.	
Page 16	But one little seal was not happy. He sat by himself. He looked sad. "What is wrong, Sammy?" said Mr. Johnson.	

Comprehension:

1) _____

_____

_____

2) _____

_____

_____

RUNNING RECORD
BENCHMARK BOOK LEVEL I

Running Record Sheet
Mama Zooms

Name _____   Date _____

144 Words   Level I   Accuracy Rate _____

PAGE	TEXT	RUNNING RECORD ANALYSIS
Page 4	Mama's got a zooming machine and she zooms me everywhere.	
Page 6	Every morning Daddy puts me in Mama's lap and we're off!	
Page 8	Mama zooms me across the lawn and she's my racehorse.	
Page 10	Mama zooms me through a puddle and she's my ship at sea.	
Page 12	Mama zooms me down a smooth sidewalk and she's my race car.	
Page 14	Mama zooms me fast down ramps. We love ramps!	
Page 16	Mama zooms me across a bridge and she's my airplane.	
Page 18	Mama zooms me through a dark hall and she's my train in a tunnel.	
Page 20	Mama zooms me over a bumpy road and she's my buckboard wagon.	
Page 22	Mama zooms me along the ocean boardwalk and she's my wave.	
Page 24	Mama has very strong arms from all our zooming.	
Page 26	Daddy and I push her up only the very steepest hills. When we get to the top, Daddy says, "See you back on earth!"…	

Comprehension:

1) _____

_____

2) _____

_____

RUNNING RECORD
BENCHMARK BOOK LEVEL J

Running Record Sheet
Poppleton Has Fun

Name _____   Date _____

129 Words   Level J   Accuracy Rate _____

PAGE	TEXT	RUNNING RECORD ANALYSIS
Page 24	Poppleton and his neighbor Cherry Sue went to a fair. There they saw quilts.	
Page 26	The quilts had pictures on them and names and buttons from people's clothes.	
Page 27	"We should make our own quilt," Poppleton said to Cherry Sue. "What fun!" said Cherry Sue. "We will ask Hudson and Fillmore to help," said Poppleton. "Perfect!" said Cherry Sue.	
Page 28	Poppleton called his friends. "We are making a quilt on Saturday," Poppleton told Hudson. "Can you come?" "Sure!" said Hudson.	
Page 30	Poppleton called Fillmore. "We are making a quilt on Saturday," said Poppleton. "Can you come?" "Certainly!" said Fillmore.	
Page 31	On Saturday everyone met at Poppleton's house. Fillmore had some old shirts. Hudson had some old trousers.	
Page 32	Poppleton had some old curtains. And Cherry Sue had a bucket of buttons. "Let's sew!" said Poppleton.	

Comprehension:

1) _____

_____

_____

2) _____

_____

_____

RUNNING RECORD
BENCHMARK BOOK LEVEL K

Running Record Sheet
The Frog Prince

Name _____   Date _____

139 Words   Level K   Accuracy Rate _____

PAGE	TEXT	RUNNING RECORD ANALYSIS
Page 5	Once upon a time there was a beautiful princess. She had a golden ball, and it was her favorite plaything. She took it wherever she went.	
Page 6	One day the princess was playing in the woods, near a well. She threw her ball high into the air. It fell—**splash!**—into the well.	
Page 7	The princess watched her golden ball sink deep into the water of the well, and she began to cry. She cried harder and harder. Suddenly someone said, "What is the matter, princess? Why are you making so much noise?"	
Page 8	The princess looked around. She looked into the well. An ugly little frog was looking up at her. The frog asked again, "What is the matter, princess?" "Oh, it's you, you old water-splasher," the princess said. "My golden ball has fallen into the well. That is why I am crying."	

Comprehension:

1) _____

_____

_____

2) _____

_____

_____

RUNNING RECORD
BENCHMARK BOOK LEVEL L

Running Record Sheet
Miss Nelson Has a Field Day

Name _____   Date _____

153 Words   Level L   Accuracy Rate _____

PAGE	TEXT	RUNNING RECORD ANALYSIS
Page 3	For some weeks now, gloom had blanketed the Horace B. Smedley School. No one laughed or threw spitballs. No one even smiled. Miss Nelson was worried.	
Page 4	Everyone was down in the dumps. Even the cafeteria ladies had lost their sparkle.	
Page 5	Mr. Blandsworth was so depressed he hid under his desk. "It's the worst team in the whole state," he said.	
Page 6	And it was true—the Smedley Tornadoes were just pitiful. They hadn't won a game all year.	
Page 7	They hadn't scored even a single point. And lately they seemed only interested in horsing around and in giving Coach the business. "Why practice?" they said. "We'll only lose anyway."	
Page 8	"We're in for it now," said old Pop Hanson, the janitor. "The big Thanksgiving game is coming up, and the Werewolves from Central are real animals. They'll make mincemeat out of our team." "What's to be done?" said Miss Nelson. "We need a real expert," said Pop.	

Comprehension:

1)_____

_____

2)_____

_____

RUNNING RECORD
BENCHMARK BOOK LEVEL M

Running Record Sheet
Dancing With the Indians

Name _____   Date _____

118 Words   Level M   Accuracy Rate _____

PAGE	TEXT	RUNNING RECORD ANALYSIS
Page 6	Mama's packed our supper, the sheep are in their pens, it's time to go and visit the Seminole Indians.	
Page 8	Golden threads of sunlight trickle through the trees turning leaves above us into lacy canopies.	
Page 9	We hear about our grandpa, as our wagon creaks along, living with the Indians because slavery was wrong.	
Page 10	He worked on a plantation before he ran away, traveling by night, hiding by day.	
Page 11	Seminoles rescued Grandpa, making him their friend, calling him blood brother, Black and Indian. Each year we go to visit, honoring those he knew, joining in the dancing, watching what they do.	
Page 12	Our wagon nears the camp. Drums pound and move our feet. Soon everyone is swaying to the tom-tom beat.	

Comprehension:

1) _____

_____

2) _____

_____

RUNNING RECORD
BENCHMARK BOOK LEVEL N

Running Record Sheet
Suitcase

Name _____   Date _____

119 Words   Level N   Accuracy Rate _____

PAGE	TEXT	RUNNING RECORD ANALYSIS
Page 34	Xander walked from school through the park. He passed the flying rings, the hand-over-hand ladder, and the trapeze. None of these interested him. He made his way to a wire stretched close to the ground. This wire was used to increase balance skills. Xander called it "the steady tester." As he came closer to the wire he was surprised to see Jeff there with a group of men.	
Page 35	Xander moved to watch as, one at a time, the men tried to walk across the wire. He stood in awe, even though their arms flailed and they fell off almost immediately. As many times as he had tried, he had never even been able to get on the wire.	

Comprehension:

1) _____

_____

_____

2) _____

_____

_____

RUNNING RECORD
BENCHMARK BOOK LEVEL O

Running Record Sheet
Chocolate Fever

Name _____   Date _____

115 Words   Level O   Accuracy Rate _____

PAGE	TEXT	RUNNING RECORD ANALYSIS
Page 34	In later years, Henry couldn't remember who screamed first. All he could recall was that both he and Mrs. Kimmelfarber were yelling their heads off. And that Nurse Molly Farthing was as cool as a cantaloupe. "Calm down now, both of you," she said. "Mrs. Kimmelfarber, you go and call Mrs. Green on the telephone. Tell her we're taking Henry to the City Hospital." Mrs. Kimmelfarber didn't move. She just stood there with her mouth open, staring at Henry.	
Page 35	"You scoot now," insisted Nurse Farthing in a stern tone. "Shoosh… off with you!" "And you, Henry Green," she said as Mrs. Kimmelfarber left the room, "are coming with me. Let us go. Quietly. Calmly."	

Comprehension:

1) _____

_____

_____

_____

2) _____

_____

_____

_____

RUNNING RECORD
BENCHMARK BOOK LEVEL P

Running Record Sheet
Who Stole The Wizard of Oz?

Name _____   Date _____

130 Words   Level P   Accuracy Rate _____

PAGE	TEXT	RUNNING RECORD ANALYSIS
Page 3	My sister Becky and I were stretched out on the front porch one morning thinking out loud about how we should spend our summer vacation. It was too hot to do much more. At about nine-thirty, a police car turned down our street, then stopped in front of the Checkertown Library. Checkertown, Ohio—that's our town. Anyway, we watched the policeman go into the library, then we went back to making plans. But half an hour later, the phone rang. Becky jumped up, ran inside, and grabbed it. "Hello?" "Is this Becky?" "Yes." "This is Mrs. Brattle. The Checkertown librarian."	
Page 4	"Oh, hi." "Becky, there's a policeman here who wants to talk to you. Can you come over now?" "What for?" "There's been a robbery at the library, Becky," said Mrs. Brattle.	

Comprehension:

1) _____

_____

2) _____

_____

RUNNING RECORD
BENCHMARK BOOK LEVEL Q

Running Record Sheet
Just Juice

Name _____   Date _____

161 Words   Level Q   Accuracy Rate _____

PAGE	TEXT	RUNNING RECORD ANALYSIS
Page 32	Someone is knocking on the front door, but we ignore it. No one but salesmen ever come calling round front. And besides, we are in the back, dancing to Pa's fiddle. Pa fiddles whenever Ma asks. Ma says it soothes her nerves and makes that teensy baby inside her settle right on down. Wait till that baby comes out and finds Pa's fiddle isn't supposed to settle anything down. Pa's fiddle swings us. It sends us sashaying across the kitchen floor. But it does not settle us down.	
Page 33	I don't know how long the person knocks around front. Finally a face appears at the back door. "Mrs. Faulstich?" Ma makes her way across the kitchen. "Mrs. Faulstich, my name is Geneva Long. Is this a good time for a visit?" Geneva Long is a big woman. Nearly as big as Ma. Ma says, "Come on, come right on in, Geneva." For a stranger, Geneva sure looks at home in our kitchen.	

Comprehension:

1) _____

_____

_____

2) _____

_____

_____

RUNNING RECORD
BENCHMARK BOOK LEVEL R

Running Record Sheet
The Trumpet of the Swan

Name _____   Date _____

167 Words   Level R   Accuracy Rate _____

PAGE	TEXT	RUNNING RECORD ANALYSIS
Page 15	One day, almost a week later, the swan slipped quietly into her nest and laid an egg. Each day she tried to deposit one egg in the nest. Sometimes she succeeded, sometimes she didn't. There were now three eggs, and she was ready to lay a fourth. As she sat there, with her husband, the cob, floating gracefully nearby, she had a strange feeling that she was being watched. It made her uneasy. Birds don't like to be stared at. They particularly dislike being stared at when they are on a nest. So the swan twisted and turned and peered everywhere. She gazed intently at the point of land that jutted out into the pond near the nest. With her sharp eyes, she searched the nearby shore for signs of an intruder. What she finally saw gave her the surprise of her life. There, seated on a log on the point of land, was a small boy. He was being very quiet, and he had no gun.	

Comprehension:

1) _____

_____

_____

2) _____

_____

_____

RUNNING RECORD
BENCHMARK BOOK LEVEL S

Running Record Sheet
Granny Torrelli Makes Soup

Name _____   Date _____

154 Words   Level S   Accuracy Rate _____

PAGE	TEXT	RUNNING RECORD ANALYSIS
Page 7	Why I liked Bailey in the first place: Bailey was always there, born next door to me, one week after me, the two of us just two babies growing up side by side, our mothers together, and me and Bailey together, on the lawn, on the porch, on the floor, playing with pots and pans and mud and worms and snow and rain and puddles. *Help Bailey* was what our mothers said to me. *Help him, will you, Rosie?* And I did. I always helped Bailey. He was my buddy, my pal, my friend. Went to the zoo, went to the park, had birthdays together.	
Page 8	What a smile that Bailey had! He was smiling mostly all the time, his hands waving out in front of him, sweeping the air. Freckles on his face, sticking-up hair very soft, very quiet Bailey boy, but not too quiet, and not pushy, not selfish, not mean, not usually.	

Comprehension:

1) _____

_____

_____

_____

2) _____

_____

_____

_____

RUNNING RECORD
BENCHMARK BOOK LEVEL T

Running Record Sheet
The Power of Un

Name _____   Date _____

147 Words   Level T   Accuracy Rate _____

PAGE	TEXT	RUNNING RECORD ANALYSIS
Page 35	I grabbed Roxy and covered her mouth as the nearby woods came alive with the scuttlings and flutterings of unseen creatures. My own heart banged against my ribs. There's nothing like the sound of pure terror to get your blood fizzing with adrenaline. "Who's there?" I said, trying hard to keep my voice steady. "Gib? It's just me, Ash!" I let the breath out of my lungs in a long, deep rush. It wasn't all relief. Some of it was embarrassment. My flashlight beam came to rest on Ash's familiar freckled face and well-worn Giants baseball cap. He was laughing. "Hey, it's not funny, all right?" I said. "You shouldn't sneak up on people in the dark." Then, realizing how	
Page 36	wimpy that sounded, I went on in a hurry. "I mean, not me. Little kids like Roxy. You could give her nightmares doing that kind of stuff."	

Comprehension:

1) _____

_____

_____

2) _____

_____

_____

RUNNING RECORD
BENCHMARK BOOK LEVEL U

Running Record Sheet
Tangerine

Name _____   Date _____

156 Words   Level U   Accuracy Rate _____

PAGE	TEXT	RUNNING RECORD ANALYSIS
Page 84	The *Tangerine Times* printed a special pullout section on the Lake Windsor Middle School sinkhole. The photos were spectacular. They had one huge shot of the splintered walkways sticking up in all directions, like Godzilla had just trampled through there. The newspaper ran a letter from Mrs. Gates to the parents of all seventh and eighth graders. We're all supposed to attend a special disaster meeting on Friday night at seven-thirty in the high school gymnasium. The letter said that "state and county officials are planning to attend," and that "they are currently working out an emergency relocation plan that will be presented at this meeting." I'll bet they are. Think about it: There are 25 portables that are completely trashed, completely out of commission. Let's say there are 25 kids assigned to each of those portables. And each kid has 7 class periods a day. That's 625 kids and 175 class periods to relocate. Awesome.	

Comprehension:

1) _____

_____

_____

_____

2) _____

_____

_____

_____

RUNNING RECORD
BENCHMARK BOOK LEVEL V

Running Record Sheet
The Firework-Maker's Daughter

Name _____   Date _____

156 Words   Level V   Accuracy Rate _____

PAGE	TEXT	RUNNING RECORD ANALYSIS
Page 55	She pulled herself up with shaking arms, and stepped inside. The floor was baking hot and the air was hardly breathable. She walked on, deeper into the earth, deeper than the moonlight went, and heard nothing but silence, and saw nothing but dark rock. Harsh, barren walls rose to left and right; she felt them with her bleeding hands. Then the tunnel opened out into a great cavern. She had never seen anything so gloomy and empty of life, and her heart sank, because she had come all this way and there was nothing here. She sank to the floor. And, as if that were a signal, a little flame licked out of the rocky wall for an instant, and went out. Then another, in a different place. Then another. Then the earth shook and groaned, and with a harsh	
Page 56	grating sound, the rocky wall tore itself open, and suddenly the cavern was full of light.	

Comprehension:

1) _____

_____

_____

2) _____

_____

_____

RUNNING RECORD
BENCHMARK BOOK LEVEL W

Running Record Sheet
Tunnels

Name _____   Date _____

152 Words   Level W   Accuracy Rate _____

PAGE	TEXT	RUNNING RECORD ANALYSIS
Page 44	The next day after school, Will and Chester resumed their work at the excavation. Will was returning from dumping the spoils, his wheelbarrow stacked high with empty buckets as he trundled to the end of the tunnel where Chester was hacking away at the stone layer. "How's it going?" Will asked him. "It's not getting any easier, that's for sure," Chester replied, wiping the sweat from his forehead with a dirty sleeve and smearing dirt across his face in the process. "Hang on, let me have a look. You take a break." "OK." Will shone his helmet lamp over the rock surface, the subtle browns and yellows of the strata gouged randomly by the tip of the pickax, and sighed loudly. "I think we'd better stop and think about this for a minute. No point banging our heads on a sandstone wall! Let's have a drink." "Yeah, good idea," Chester said gratefully.	

Comprehension:

1) _____

_____

_____

2) _____

_____

_____

RUNNING RECORD
BENCHMARK BOOK LEVEL X

Running Record Sheet
A Break With Charity

Name _____   Date _____

152 Words   Level X   Accuracy Rate _____

PAGE	TEXT	RUNNING RECORD ANALYSIS
Page 32	The hour was late by the time I got to Salem Town, where candlelight from all the house windows threw a soft glow out on darkened streets. I knew I was in trouble, for in the cart I still had many of the items I was supposed to have distributed to the poor of Salem Village: precious packets of needles and skeins of wool, an iron cook pot or two, bolts of warm flannel, some molasses, flour, and salted codfish. Mama would want to know why I had returned with my cargo. And so it was that I determined to lie. I was not practiced in the art of dissembling, the word given to such a sin. There had been no need in	
Page 33	my life, up until now, to keep any of my doings from my parents. But in the next few months I was to learn the art of dissembling well.	

Comprehension:

1) _____

_____

_____

_____

2) _____

_____

_____

_____

RUNNING RECORD
BENCHMARK BOOK LEVEL Y

Running Record Sheet
Larklight

Name _____   Date _____

143 Words   Level Y   Accuracy Rate _____

PAGE	TEXT	RUNNING RECORD ANALYSIS
Page 35	We saw no more of the spiders as we flew down the stairs to the lifeboat house. We knew the lifeboats well, for Father had made us practise in them lest there should ever be a fire at Larklight. They were barrel-shaped objects, squatting on	
Page 36	spring-loaded projector plates in the middle of the shadowy boathouse. We checked about nervously for spiders before we heaved open the hatch of the nearer one and pulled ourselves inside. 'Are we to wait for Father?' wondered Myrtle, but she was looking very solemnly at me, as though she already knew the answer. I shook my head. 'Were there a very great number of those awful creatures?' she asked. I nodded. 'And did they devour him?' Myrtle whispered. I shrugged, and shook her away when she said, 'Poor Art! Then we are orphans!' and tried to hug me.	

Comprehension:

1) _____

_____

_____

2) _____

_____

_____

RUNNING RECORD
BENCHMARK BOOK LEVEL Z

Running Record Sheet
Harry Potter and the Deathly Hallows

Name _____   Date _____

170 Words   Level Z   Accuracy Rate _____

PAGE	TEXT	RUNNING RECORD ANALYSIS
Page 350	Without realizing it, he was digging his fingers into his arms as if he were trying to resist physical pain. He had spilled his own blood more times than he could count; he had lost all the bones in his right arm once; this journey had already given him scars to his chest and forearm to join those on his hand and forehead, but never, until this moment, had he felt himself to be fatally weakened, vulnerable, and naked, as though the best part of his magical power had been torn from him. He knew exactly what Hermione would say if he	
Page 351	expressed any of this: The wand is only as good as the wizard. But she was wrong; his case was different. She had not felt the wand spin like the needle of a compass and shoot golden flames at his enemy. He had lost the protection of the twin cores, and only now that it was gone did he realize how much he had been counting upon it.	

Comprehension:

1) _____

_____

_____

2) _____

_____

_____

GUIDELINES FOR **ASSESSING** READING COMPREHENSION THROUGH **RETELLING**

Select similar texts.	When comparing a student's retelling over time, use the same type of text each time. Compare narratives with other narratives and nonfiction texts with other nonfiction texts. Also select similar levels unless you are purposely moving a struggling reader down a level to discover an independent reading level or moving a reader up to a more challenging level.
Prepare a guide sheet.	In preparation for retelling, preview a text to determine what kinds of ideas and information you will be listening for in the student retelling. You may want to create a guide sheet or checklist that you can refer to and use for taking notes.

For fiction texts, include on your checklist:

- **title and author name**
- **genre**
- **character names and a note whether they are major or minor characters**
- **note about the setting, including any changes in setting**
- **brief description of the problem, conflict, or goal in the story**
- **list of important events in sequential order in the beginning, middle, and end**
- **brief description of how the problem or conflict is solved, or the goal reached**

For nonfiction texts, include on your checklist:

- **title and author name**
- **genre**
- **book topic**
- **main idea of the book and of any sections or chapters**
- **important details that support main ideas**
- **important people included if the book is a narrative**
- **important events listed in sequential order**
- **text features such as photographs or illustrations, diagrams, charts, and maps**

Ask the student to retell the text.	Make sure the student has recently read the text selected for the retelling. Then ask the student to retell the story or information, starting at the beginning and telling what happened or what the author said about the topic. As the student retells, make checks or notes on your guide sheet that will help you recall what the student included and the sequence of information. If you find it difficult to make checks or notes, it may be because the student is retelling information out of sequential order, has omitted important ideas, is focusing on unimportant information, or has not comprehended the main idea or the plot. For events or information told out of sequence, you may want to number the order of ideas students express instead of just checking them off.

Listen for what the student says and does not say.

When you listen to a retelling, listen for what the student says and how the student retells a fiction or nonfiction text. What the student leaves out is as important as what he or she says as an indicator of comprehension and understanding.

In a fiction retelling, listen for:

- **characters' names**
- **important events in sequence**
- **important details**
- **use of language and vocabulary from the story**
- **understanding of how the story is organized**
- **understanding of the genre, such as whether a student knows a story is realistic, a fantasy, or a special type of literature such as a folktale, fable, or mystery, as evidenced by mention of setting, understanding that characters are imaginary, connection with realistic situations and people, or a description of clues that lead to solving a mystery**

In a nonfiction retelling, listen for:

- **statement of what the text is about**
- **statements of main ideas**
- **key ideas and facts**
- **mention of text features from which the student derived information, such as a photograph or illustration, chart, diagram, or map**
- **use of language and vocabulary from the text**
- **understanding of the genre, such as whether the student points out that the text describes or explains a topic, tells about the life of a person or is told by that person, or narrates an important time or event in history**
- **understanding of how the text is organized by mention of details that support main ideas, or how the author explained or described a topic, presented a problem and solution, showed causes and effects, or compared and contrasted people, things, or ideas**

Provide prompts if needed.

When a student is retelling, let him finish without prompting for information. If the retelling is incomplete, out of order, or leaves out important information, you may want to prompt with more specific questions about parts of the text the student misunderstood or did not include. Note how many prompts are needed to complete the retelling.

Summarize and evaluate the retelling.

Using your guide sheet, discuss and review the retelling with the student to help her understand what can be improved and how. This process also helps you develop instructional goals for future sessions.

You can also use your guide sheet to help you evaluate the retelling at a later time and determine what level the student is on and what instruction she needs. Keep your guide sheets for each student retelling to give you information for determining student progress and points for intervention.

Evaluating Students' Retellings

Students' retellings of fiction and nonfiction will give you a snapshot of where students fall in their ability to process and comprehend text. The following criteria for establishing levels can aid you in placing a student at a particular level and help you plan for instruction.

FICTION

Level	Criteria for Establishing Level
3	Most-complete retellings: • Indicate an understanding of the genre through description of and connections made to setting, characters, and plot • Present a sequence of actions and events • Provide explanations for the motivations behind characters' actions • Include character names • Elaborate using important details from the story • Comment on or evaluate the story • Do not require prompts during retelling
2	Less complex retellings: • Indicate a basic understanding of genre in brief comments of characters, setting, and plot • Present concrete events in sequence • Supply missing information through appropriate inferences • Include some explanation of the causes of events or characters' motivations • Include some important details • Require one or two prompts during retelling
1	Simple descriptive retellings: • Are partial or limited • Indicate a lack of awareness of genre through no mention of a genre's features • Have simple beginning, middle, and end • May include events out of sequence • May describe a setting • Present an initiating event and the outcome of a problem • Include misinterpretations • Refer to characters as "he" or "she" rather than by name • Require three or more prompts during retelling

NONFICTION

Level	Criteria for Establishing Level
3	Most-complete retellings: • Show a comprehension of the topic • Indicate an understanding of the genre in a description of the text, its purpose, and how it is organized • Present main ideas of whole text and parts of text • Provide important details that support main ideas • Include key ideas and facts • Elaborate using details enhanced by prior knowledge • Comment on or evaluate the text • Do not require prompts during retelling
2	Less complex retellings: • Show a basic comprehension of the topic • Indicate a basic understanding of the genre and text organization in a description of the book • Present concrete related facts or events in sequence • Supply missing information through appropriate inferences • Include some main ideas • Provide some important details that support main ideas • Mention some key ideas and facts, but omit others • Require one or two prompts during retelling
1	Simple descriptive retellings: • Are partial or limited • Provide the topic of the text • Include misinterpretations • Include general ideas without focusing on specific main ideas • Omit important details to support main ideas • Do not include comments on text structure • Require three or more prompts during retelling

BENCHMARK BOOKS

Level	Benchmark Book
Level A	Helping
Level B	Off to the City
Level C	The Big Blue Sea
Level D	The Little Red Hen
Level E	Fred's Wish for Fish
Level F	The Country Mouse and the Town Mouse
Level G	Justin's New Bike
Level H	Sammy the Seal
Level I	Mama Zooms
Level J	Poppleton Has Fun
Level K	The Frog Prince
Level L	Miss Nelson Has a Field Day
Level M	Dancing With the Indians
Level N	Suitcase
Level O	Chocolate Fever
Level P	Who Stole *The Wizard of Oz*?
Level Q	Just Juice
Level R	The Trumpet of the Swan
Level S	Granny Torrelli Makes Soup
Level T	The Power of Un
Level U	Tangerine
Level V	The Firework-Maker's Daughter
Level W	Tunnels
Level X	A Break With Charity
Level Y	Larklight
Level Z	Harry Potter and the Deathly Hallows

READING LEVEL CORRELATIONS*

Grade Level (Basal)	Guided Reading Levels	DRA Levels	Success For All Levels	Reading Recovery Levels	Stages of Reading	Lexiles	DRP Text
Kindergarten	A B	A 2	1–3	A–B, 2	Emergent		
Pre-Primer	C D E	3–4 6 8	4–25 25	3–4 5–6 7–8	Emergent/ Early	BR–200	
Primer	F G	10 12	26–27	9–10 12	Early/ Transitional	200–300	
1st Grade	H I	14 16	38–48	14 16	Early/ Transitional	300–400	25–30
2nd Grade	J–K L–M	16–18 20–24	2.0	18 20	Transitional Fluency/ Extending	400–550	30–44
3rd Grade	N O–P	28–30 34–38	3.0	22 24	Fluency/ Extending	600–700	44–54
4th Grade	Q–R	40	4.0	26	Fluency/ Extending Advanced	750–900	46–55
5th Grade	S–V	50	—	26–28	Fluency/ Extending Advanced	850–950	49–57
6th Grade	W–Y Z	60 70–80	—	30 32–34	Advanced	950–1050	51–60

*See **Text Gradient Chart** on the back of your materials folder. This chart identifies the overlapping level ranges for each grade in the *Scholastic Guided Reading Program.*

USING THE GUIDED READING PROGRAM

Characteristics of Text

The easiest books are included in Levels A and B. We suggest that children begin using Level A books for guided reading after they have listened to many stories and participated in shared reading. They should have some familiarity with print and understand that you read print and move from left to right in doing so. Children need not know all the letters of the alphabet and their sounds before reading Level A books.

Level A includes picture books without words, some with simple labels or captions, and some with as many as five or six words, often on one line.

In general, these books have clear, easy-to-read print with generous space between words. These simple formats enable young children to focus on print and reading from left to right, while gradually increasing their control over more words. Many of the books have high-frequency words and repeating language patterns. Print is presented in a variety of ways, which helps children become flexible readers from the start. In general, the books focus on topics that are familiar to most children. Books with more complex topics usually have fewer words and will require more of an introduction and teacher-child interaction to support understanding.

Behaviors to Notice and Support

	Child's Name						
Understands familiar concepts in stories and illustrations							
Differentiates print from pictures							
Holds the book and turns pages from right to left							
Reads words from left to right							
Begins to match word by word, pointing with one finger under words							
Locates both known and new words							
Remembers and uses language patterns							
Relates the book to his/her experience							

USING THE
GUIDED READING PROGRAM

Characteristics of Text

Level B books generally have simple story lines or a single idea. The print is easy to read, with adequate space between words so that children can point to words as they read. Books at this level generally have one or two lines of print on a page, somewhat longer sentences, and a variety of punctuation.

There is direct correspondence between the text and pictures, and repeating patterns support the reader. Topics are generally familiar to most children. If more complex concepts are involved, the reading of the book will require teacher-child interaction to support understanding.

Behaviors to Notice and Support

Child's Name							
Demonstrates control of left-to-right movement and return sweep							
Begins to control word-by-word matching across two lines of text, pointing with one finger							
Notices and interprets detail in pictures							
Talks about ideas in the text							
Remembers and uses language patterns in text							
Uses knowledge of high-frequency words to check on reading							
Uses word-by-word matching to check on reading							
Notices mismatches in meaning or language							
Uses visual information, such as the first letter of the word, to read known and new words							
Pays close attention to print							
Notices features of letters and words							
Begins to self-monitor, noticing mismatches in meaning or language							
Rereads to confirm or figure out new words							

USING THE
GUIDED READING PROGRAM

Characteristics of Text

Level C books have simple story lines and topics that are familiar to most children. Some may offer a new viewpoint on a familiar topic. Level C books generally have more words and lines of print than books at earlier levels. Print is clear and readable, with adequate space between words. Most sentences are simple, but some have more complex structure, offering readers a challenge. While Level C books include some repeating language patterns, these are more complex and there is a shift to more varied patterns. Language patterns are more likely to change from page to page, so children cannot rely on them to make predictions and must pay closer attention to print. Level C books include many high-frequency words, as well as easily decodable words.

Behaviors to Notice and Support

	Child's Name						
Demonstrates control of left-to-right directionality and word-by-word matching across several lines of print							
Begins to track print with eyes							
Rereads to solve problems, such as figuring out new words							
Demonstrates awareness of punctuation by pausing and using some phrasing							
Uses picture details to help figure out words							
Remembers and uses language patterns in text							
Rereads to confirm or figure out new words							
Solves some new words independently							
Controls directionality and word-by-word matching with eyes, using finger at points of difficulty							
Uses visual information to predict, check, and confirm reading							
Recognizes known words quickly and uses them to figure out the meaning of new words							
Searches for understanding while reading							

USING THE
GUIDED READING PROGRAM

Characteristics of Text

Stories at Level D are slightly more complex than at previous levels. Generally, Level D books have topics that are familiar to most children, but also include some abstract or unfamiliar ideas. Text layout is still easy to follow, with both large and small print. Sentences are a little longer than at Level C. Some are carried over to the next page or several pages and use a full range of punctuation. There are more compound words, multisyllabic words, and words with a variety of inflectional endings. Illustrations are still supportive, but less so than at the previous level, requiring the reader to pay more attention to print.

Behaviors to Notice and Support

	Child's Name							
Remembers language patterns and repeating events over longer stretches of text								
Self-corrects, using visual information								
Controls directionality and word-by-word matching with eyes, using finger only at points of difficulty								
Searches for understanding while reading								
Remembers details from the text and pictures								
Pays close attention to words and their structural features (for example, endings)								
Reads fluently, with phrasing								
Rereads to confirm or figure out new words								
Solves new words using knowledge of sound/letter relationships and word parts								

USING THE
GUIDED READING PROGRAM

Characteristics of Text

Level E books are generally longer than books at previous levels, with either more pages or more lines of text on a page. Some have sentences that carry over several pages and have a full range of punctuation. The text structure is generally more complex: stories have more or longer episodes,

and informational books have more difficult ideas and concepts. However, in texts with more difficult concepts, there are usually repeating language patterns that offer some support. There are more multisyllabic and compound words at this level.

Behaviors to Notice and Support

	Child's Name							
Tracks print with eyes except at points of difficulty								
Uses language syntax and meaning to read fluently, with phrasing								
Demonstrates awareness of punctuation by pausing, phrasing, and reading with inflection								
Rereads to self-monitor or self-correct phrasing and expression								
Recognizes many words quickly and automatically								
Figures out some longer words by taking them apart								
Relates texts to others previously read								
Reads for meaning but checks with the visual aspects of print (letters, sounds, words)								
Rereads to search for meaning and accuracy								
Remembers details and uses them to clarify meaning								
Demonstrates understanding by talking about text after reading								

USING THE GUIDED READING PROGRAM

Characteristics of Text

In general, texts at Level F are longer and have more story episodes than at previous levels. There are also shorter texts with some unusual language patterns. Books have some concepts unfamiliar to children and some are even abstract, requiring reflection. Pictures continue to support reading, but closer attention to print is required. Language patterns are more characteristic of written language than of spoken language. Some Level F books have smaller print and more words and lines of text. There are many more new words and a greater variety of high-frequency words. A full range of punctuation is used to enhance meaning.

Behaviors to Notice and Support

	Child's Name							
Tracks print with eyes, using the finger only at points of difficulty								
Demonstrates awareness of punctuation by pausing, phrasing, and reading with inflection								
Uses syntax of written language to figure out new words and their meaning								
Uses sound/letter relationships, word parts, and other visual information to figure out new words								
Uses known words to figure out new words								
Uses multiple sources of information to search and self-correct								
Figures out longer words while reading for meaning								
Rereads to figure out words, self-correct, or improve phrasing and expression								
Rereads to search for meaning								
Recognizes most words quickly and automatically								
Moves quickly through the text								
Reads fluently, with phrasing								
Talks about ideas in the text and relates them to his/her experiences and to other texts								

USING THE
GUIDED READING PROGRAM

Characteristics of Text

Most books at Level G are not repetitive. These books include a variety of patterns. Knowledge of punctuation is important in understanding what the sentence means and how it should be spoken. Vocabulary is more challenging, with a greater range of words and more difficult words, including some that are technical and require content knowledge. Concepts and ideas may be less familiar than at previous levels. Level G books have a greater variety of styles of print and text layout, requiring close attention to print and flexibility on the part of the reader.

Behaviors to Notice and Support

	Child's Name						
Reads fluently and rapidly, with appropriate phrasing							
Follows print with eyes, occasionally using finger at points of difficulty							
Notices and uses punctuation to assist smooth reading							
Recognizes most words quickly and automatically							
Uses sound/letter relationships, known words, and word parts to figure out new words							
Uses meaning, visual information, and language syntax to figure out words							
Rereads to figure out words, self-correct, or improve phrasing and expression							
Rereads to search for meaning							
Remembers details to support the accumulation of meaning throughout the text							
Uses pictures for information but does not rely on them to make predictions							

USING THE
GUIDED READING PROGRAM

Characteristics of Text

Level H books are similar in difficulty to Level G, but Level H has a wider variety, including books with poetic or literary language. Sentences vary in length and difficulty, and some complex sentences carry over several pages. Children will need to be familiar with the syntactic patterns that occur.

Books have fewer repeating events and language patterns, requiring more control of aspects of print. The vocabulary is expanded and includes words that are less frequently used in oral language. The size of print varies widely.

Behaviors to Notice and Support

	Child's Name							
Reads fluently and rapidly, with appropriate phrasing								
Follows the text with eyes, using finger only at points of particular difficulty								
Notices and uses punctuation to assist smooth reading								
Recognizes most words rapidly								
Uses sound/letter relationships, known words, and word parts to figure out new words								
Uses meaning, visual information, and language syntax to solve problems								
Rereads phrases to figure out words, self-correct, or improve phrasing and expression								
Rereads to search for meaning								
Remembers details to support meaning accumulated through the text								
Uses pictures for information but does not rely on them to make predictions								
Searches for meaning while reading, stopping to think or talk about ideas								

USING THE
GUIDED READING PROGRAM

Characteristics of Text

In general, the books at Level I are longer and more complex than at Levels G and H. The size of print is smaller and there are many more lines of print on the page. Books have longer sentences and paragraphs. There are more multisyllabic words, requiring complex word-solving skills. This level offers a greater variety of texts, including some that are informational, with technical language. Events in the text are more highly elaborated. Illustrations enhance the story, but provide low support for understanding meaning.

Behaviors to Notice and Support

Child's Name								
Actively figures out new words, using a range of strategies								
Follows the print with eyes								
Reads fluently, slowing down to figure out new words and then resuming speed								
Begins to silently read some of the text								
In oral reading, rereads some words or phrases to self-correct or improve expression								
Rereads to search for meaning								
Flexibly uses meaning, language syntax, and visual information to figure out new words and to monitor reading								
Self-corrects errors that cause loss of meaning								
Rereads when necessary to self-correct, but not as a habit								
Demonstrates understanding of the story and characters								
Goes beyond the text in discussions and interpretations								
Sustains problem solving and development of meaning through a longer text and over a two- or three-day period								

USING THE GUIDED READING PROGRAM

Characteristics of Text

Although it supports essentially the same reading behaviors, Level J offers books that are more difficult and varied than those at Level I. It includes informational books with new concepts and beginning chapter books with complex narratives and memorable characters. The amount of print varies; some Level J books have full pages of text with few illustrations. Generally, illustrations enhance the text but offer little support for understanding text meaning or figuring out new words. The difficulty of the language also varies. There are books with easy and familiar language and others with literary language or other challenges. Texts have many high-frequency words but may also have unfamiliar and/or technical words.

Behaviors to Notice and Support

	Child's Name							
Uses multiple sources of information to process text smoothly								
Uses multiple strategies to figure out new words while focusing on meaning								
Analyzes words from left to right, using knowledge of sound/letter relationships								
Uses known words and word parts to figure out new words								
Reads fluently, slowing down to figure out new words and then resuming speed								
Flexibly uses meaning, language syntax, and visual information to monitor reading								
Self-corrects errors that cause loss of meaning								
Rereads when necessary to self-correct, but not as a habit								
Rereads to search for meaning								
Demonstrates understanding of the story and characters								
Goes beyond the text in discussions and interpretations								
Sustains problem-solving and development of meaning through a longer text read over several days								
Silently reads sections of text								
Makes inferences, predicts, and analyzes character and plot								

USING THE GUIDED READING PROGRAM

Characteristics of Text

The Level K collection includes longer chapter books with memorable characters, shorter informational books with technical language and new concepts, and literary texts with illustrations that enhance meaning. Stories have multiple episodes related to a single plot. Some stories have to do with times, places, and characters outside children's experience.

Readers will need to use a variety of strategies to figure out new writing styles. At this level, most reading will be silent, although teachers will always sample oral reading or invite children to read aloud for emphasis or enjoyment in group sessions. It will take more than one sitting for children to read some of the longer chapter books.

Behaviors to Notice and Support

	Child's Name						
Integrates multiple sources of information while reading with fluency							
When reading orally, reads rapidly, with phrasing, slowing down to problem solve and then resuming speed							
Reads silently much of the time							
Demonstrates understanding of the text after silent reading							
Makes inferences, predicts, and analyzes character and plot							
Flexibly uses multiple word-solving strategies while focusing on meaning							
Goes beyond the text in understanding of problems and characters							
Demonstrates facility in interpreting the text							
Sustains attention to meaning and interpretation of a longer text read over several days							

USING THE
GUIDED READING PROGRAM

Characteristics of Text

In general, reading behaviors for Level L are the same as for Level K except they are applied to longer and/or more complex books. At Level L there is greater variety of texts, including informational books, biographies, chapter books, and some longer, highly literary, or informational picture books.

Chapter books have more sophisticated plots and characters that are developed throughout the text. Some books have abstract or symbolic themes that require higher-level conceptual understandings. Texts contain an expanded vocabulary with many multisyllabic words.

Behaviors to Notice and Support

	Child's Name							
Integrates multiple sources of information while reading with fluency								
When reading orally, reads rapidly, with phrasing								
Reads orally, with accuracy, not stopping to self-correct in the interest of fluency and phrasing								
In oral reading, uses multiple word-solving strategies with longer words								
Reads silently most of the time								
Demonstrates understanding and facility in interpreting the text after silent reading								
After reading longer sections of a text, predicts events, outcomes, problem resolutions, and character changes								
Makes connections between the text read and other books								
Sustains attention to meaning and interpretation of a longer text read over several days								

USING THE
GUIDED READING PROGRAM

Characteristics of Text

Level M books have a variety of formats. Topics vary widely, and include subjects that will be familiar to students as well as those that are new. Literary selections have complex language and subtle meanings that require interpretation and background knowledge.

Chapter books are longer with few pictures. This requires readers to have mastery of the text. Many books have small print and little space between words. Vocabulary is expanded, and many words require background knowledge for comprehension.

Behaviors to Notice and Support

Behaviors to Notice and Support	Student's Name						
Uses multiple sources of information to figure out words rapidly while focusing on meaning							
Flexibly applies word-solving strategies to more-complex, multisyllabic words							
Demonstrates facility in interpreting text while reading orally, with fluency and phrasing							
Reads orally with high accuracy in most instances, not stopping to self-correct errors in the interest of fluency and phrasing							
Reads silently, except during assessment or to demonstrate text interpretation							
After reading longer sections of text, predicts outcomes, problem resolutions, and character changes							
Remembers details and sustains attention to meaning through a longer text							
Demonstrates understanding and facility at interpretation after silent reading							
Makes connections between the text read and other books							
Goes beyond the text to make more sophisticated interpretations							

USING THE
GUIDED READING PROGRAM

Characteristics of Text

The Level N collection includes longer texts in a variety of genres. There are chapter books that present memorable characters developed through literary devices such as humor, irony, and whimsy. There are informational books and books that offer mystery and suspense. Level N also has shorter selections that provide opportunity to interpret texts and go beyond them. Vocabulary continues to expand, and topics go well beyond students' own experience.

Behaviors to Notice and Support

	Student's Name							
Uses multiple strategies to figure out new words quickly								
Demonstrates facility in text interpretation while reading orally, with fluency and phrasing								
Reads silently, except during assessment or when demonstrating text interpretation								
Remembers details from one section of text to the next								
Sustains attention to a longer text, remembering details and revising interpretations								
Notices how illustrations convey the author's meaning								
Demonstrates sophisticated interpretation of characters and plot								
Makes connections among a wide variety of texts								
Goes beyond the text to speculate on alternative meanings								

USING THE
GUIDED READING PROGRAM

Characteristics of Text

Books at Level O include selections from children's literature and chapter books. Books at this level explore more mature themes and topics that go beyond students' experience and expand it. Students can empathize with characters and learn about the lives of others. The vocabulary is sophisticated and varied. Most words will be known or within students' control; however, many will require interpretation of meaning. Many new multisyllabic words are included. Sentences are more complex and use a full range of punctuation.

Behaviors to Notice and Support

Student's Name							
Solves words quickly and automatically while focusing on meaning							
Searches to understand the subtle shades of meaning that words can convey							
Demonstrates facility in text interpretation while reading orally, with fluency and phrasing							
In oral reading, figures out new words rapidly while reading smoothly and expressively							
Sustains attention to a text read over several days, remembering details and revising interpretations as new events are encountered							
After reading silently, demonstrates understanding and sophistication in text interpretation							
Makes connections among texts to enhance interpretation							
Goes beyond the text to speculate on alternative meanings							
Shows the ability to summarize the text in writing							

USING THE
GUIDED READING PROGRAM

Characteristics of Text

In general, books at this level are longer and ideas and language are more complex than at previous levels. Level P has a variety of informational texts, including history and biography. Through this variety, students become familiar with texts that are organized differently and learn how to gain information from them. Other genres include chapter books that explore the problems of early adolescence.

Behaviors to Notice and Support

	Student's Name							
When reading silently, reads rapidly and with attention to meaning								
Actively acquires new vocabulary through reading								
Demonstrates facility in text interpretation while reading orally, with fluency and phrasing								
In oral reading, figures out new words rapidly while reading smoothly and expressively								
Sustains attention to a text read over many days, remembering details and revising interpretations as new events are encountered								
Demonstrates interest in reading an extended text over a longer time period								
After reading silently, demonstrates understanding and sophistication in interpreting meaning								
Compares the text with other books in an analytic way								
Goes beyond the text to speculate on alternative meanings								
Shows the ability to summarize and extend the text in writing								

USING THE
GUIDED READING PROGRAM

Characteristics of Text

Level Q includes literature selections with sophisticated humor, complex plots, and memorable characters. Themes at this level are sophisticated and require interpretation. They serve as a good foundation for group discussion. Illustrations and their relationship to the text can be examined as well. Books have complex structure and difficult words that offer challenges. There are some words from languages other than English. Longer texts require an extended time period to read.

Behaviors to Notice and Support

	Student's Name							
Reads rapidly, with attention to meaning, when reading silently								
Actively acquires new vocabulary through reading								
Demonstrates facility in text interpretation while reading orally, with fluency and phrasing								
In oral reading, figures out new words rapidly while reading smoothly and expressively								
Sustains attention to a text read over many days, remembering details and revising interpretations as new events are encountered								
Demonstrates interest in reading an extended text over a longer time period								
Uses illustrations to help analyze text meaning								
After reading silently, demonstrates understanding and sophistication in interpreting meaning								
Compares the text to other books in an analytic way								
Goes beyond the text to speculate on alternative meanings								
Goes beyond the text to interpret characters' thoughts and feelings								
Shows the ability to analyze and extend the text in writing								

USING THE
GUIDED READING PROGRAM

Characteristics of Text

At Level R, both fiction and nonfiction have a range of historical place and time settings, giving students an opportunity to empathize with characters and learn about their lives and the times and places in which they lived. In general, skills are the same as at Level Q, but are extended over a wider variety of texts. Some books require sustained reading over a longer time period. Vocabulary and language are sophisticated and offer challenges to the reader.

Behaviors to Notice and Support

	Student's Name							
Reads rapidly, both orally and silently, while focusing on meaning								
Actively acquires new vocabulary through reading								
Sustains attention to a text read over many days, remembering details and revising interpretations as new events are encountered								
Demonstrates interest in reading an extended text over a longer time period								
Extends the text in various ways, including through research								
Demonstrates interest and ability in interpreting shorter selections								
Uses illustrations to help analyze text meaning								
After reading silently, demonstrates understanding and sophistication in interpreting meaning								
Uses comparison with other texts to assist interpretation								
Goes beyond the text to interpret characters' thoughts and feelings and to speculate on alternative meanings								
Demonstrates all interpretive and analytic skills in writing								

USING THE GUIDED READING PROGRAM

Characteristics of Text

Level S includes literary selections, highly literary or informational picture books, and chapter books in a variety of genres. The collection reflects a wide variety of topics, cultures, and historical settings. Sentences and paragraphs at this level are complex.

Words present many shades of meaning which readers must interpret from the text and their own background knowledge. Selections offer opportunities for readers to make connections with other books they have read at earlier levels.

Behaviors to Notice and Support

	Student's Name						
Reads rapidly, both orally and silently, with attention to meaning							
Rapidly acquires new vocabulary through reading							
Sustains attention to a text read over many days, remembering details and revising interpretations as new events are encountered							
Demonstrates interest and ability in interpreting shorter selections							
Demonstrates flexibility in reading many different kinds of texts							
After reading silently, demonstrates understanding and sophistication in interpreting meaning							
Goes beyond the text to interpret characters' thoughts and feelings and to speculate on alternative meanings							
Demonstrates all analytic and interpretive skills in writing							
Extends text meaning through research, writing, or the arts							

USING THE
GUIDED READING PROGRAM

Characteristics of Text

The Level T collection has a great variety of genres. Short selections include informational books, legends, historical fiction, and folktales. Chapter books include autobiographies, historical narratives, realistic fiction, science fiction, and other fantasy stories. Some chapter books are quite long and require reading over an extended time. Judgment is needed as to whether students can sustain interest for these longer selections. Selections contain many sophisticated, multisyllabic words, and readers will need to consider both their literal and connotative meanings.

Behaviors to Notice and Support

	Student's Name						
Reads rapidly, both orally and silently, with attention to meaning							
In oral and silent reading, figures out new words automatically and easily interprets word meaning							
Sustains attention to a text read over many days, remembering details and revising interpretations as new events are encountered							
Demonstrates interest and ability in interpreting shorter selections							
Demonstrates flexibility in reading texts of different styles and genres							
After reading silently, demonstrates understanding and ability to analyze characters and plot							
Reflects knowledge of literary genre in conversation and writing							
Extends and demonstrates understanding of the text through writing in a variety of genres							
Extends and demonstrates understanding of the text through public speaking, research, or the arts							

USING THE GUIDED READING PROGRAM

Characteristics of Text

Text at Level U requires readers to employ a wide range of sophisticated reading strategies that approach adult levels. The difference, of course, is that elementary and middle school students are still gaining the world experience and content knowledge, or the accumulation of text experience, needed to deeply understand the more complex texts they will be reading at levels U through Z. By this time, students have built an integrated processing system, but they need to apply their strategies to increasingly difficult levels of text. As they do so, reading with fluency and understanding, they will expand and build their reading strategies.

Fiction texts at level U may have several different themes and multiple story lines. Texts are increasingly literary, with writers expressing layers of meaning through symbolism. Themes are more abstract; creative formats may be used, such as collections of short stories that build meaning over different texts, or novels that incorporate diaries, poetry, or stories within stories. Generally, there are more characters to follow and their development is more complex; there are plots and subplots. Informational texts at Level U cover a wide range of topics and present specific, technical information. As with earlier levels, illustrations require interpretation and connection to text.

Behaviors to Notice and Support

	Student's Name							
Notices graphic illustrations and gets information from them								
Synthesizes information from graphic information with the body of the text								
Uses the table of contents to help in understanding the organization of the text								
Grasps "layers" of meaning in a story; for example, specific understandings plus the "bigger picture"								
Reads, understands, and appreciates literary language								
Interprets illustrations and their connections to the text								
Keeps up with several different themes and many characters								
Interprets characters' motives and the influences on their development								
Recognizes and appreciates a wide range of genres, both fiction and nonfiction								
Notices and uses a full range of punctuation, including more rarely used forms such as dashes								
Learns technical words from reading								
Uses reading to learn about self and others								

USING THE
GUIDED READING PROGRAM

Characteristics of Text

At Level V, readers employ essentially the same range of strategies as at the previous level, but more background knowledge will be required for true understanding. Also, students will be rapidly adding to their reading vocabularies. Fiction includes science fiction that presents sophisticated ideas and concepts. In many works of realistic or historical fiction, the writer is conveying a significant message beyond the story. Readers must think critically and sustain attention, memory, and understanding of theme over much longer texts. Full appreciation of texts requires noticing aspects of the writer's craft, including metaphor, simile, and symbolism. Many long texts have print in a much smaller font. Informational texts present complex ideas and may use language that is more technical. Topics are more often distant from students' experience in time and place. Biographies provide a significant amount of historical information. Many focus on harsh themes. Other, longer biographies are told in narrative style but present complex themes.

Behaviors to Notice and Support

	Student's Name							
Understands and talks about complex themes, analyzing them and applying them to current life situations								
Understands many different perspectives that are encountered in fiction and nonfiction texts								
Evaluates both fiction and nonfiction texts for their authenticity and accuracy								
Deals with mature topics such as death, war, prejudice, and courage								
Thinks critically about and discusses the content of a literary work or the quality of writing								
Notices aspects of the writer's craft and looks at the text from a writer's point of view								
Sustains attention and thinking over the reading of texts that are long and have smaller fonts								
Tries new genres, topics, and authors, and is able to compare them with known genres, topics, and authors								
Makes connections across texts to notice an author's style or technique								
Understands symbolism in both realistic fiction and fantasy; discusses what symbols mean in terms of today's society								
Brings prior knowledge to bear in understanding literary references								
Learns technical language and concepts through reading								
Learns about self and others through reading, especially about societies that are different from one's own								

USING THE
GUIDED READING PROGRAM

Characteristics of Text

Texts at Level W have themes that explore the human condition, with the same kinds of social problems mentioned at earlier levels. Fiction and nonfiction texts present characters who suffer hardship and learn from it. The writing is sophisticated, with complex sentences, literary language, and symbolism. Texts vary in length; print is generally in a small font. Comprehending texts at this level will require awareness of social and political issues; through them, readers can learn to understand current social problems at deeper levels.

Fantasy includes science fiction as well as "high" fantasy that introduces heroic characters, questions, and contests between good and evil. Informational texts may present complex graphic information and require readers to possess a wide range of content knowledge and to understand all of the basic organizational structures for nonfiction. Narrative-style biographies include many details of their subjects' lives and prompt readers to make inferences about what motivated their achievements.

Behaviors to Notice and Support

	Student's Name						
Sustains reading over longer and more complex texts; is not intimidated by varying layouts and styles of print							
Builds understanding of a wide variety of human problems							
Uses reading to expand awareness of people who are different from oneself							
Understands and learns from characters' experiences							
Learns about self and others through reading; actively seeks understanding of people different from oneself by culture, period of history, or other variation							
Deals with mature themes such as prejudice, war, death, survival, and poverty, and is able to discuss them in relation to one's own experiences							
Understands the complexities of human characters as they develop and change; discusses one's own point of view and relationship to characters							
Integrates understandings derived from graphic illustrations and the text							
Expands world knowledge through reading							
Flexibly and automatically uses tools such as glossary, references, index, credentials for authors, legends, charts, and diagrams							

USING THE
GUIDED READING PROGRAM

Characteristics of Text

Texts at Level X include the same wide range of genres shown at previous levels, but the themes explored are increasingly mature. Fantasy depicts quests and the struggle between good and evil. High fantasy includes complex, extended symbolic narratives that require knowledge of previously read texts for full understanding. Readers are required to go substantially beyond the literal meaning of the text to construct a writer's implied meaning. In addition, texts require interpretation of theme and plot. In fiction texts, there may be many characters to follow and understand. There is a continuing increase in the sophistication of vocabulary, language, and topics. Nonfiction texts require extensive prior knowledge for full understanding. In addition, texts are designed to present a great deal of new knowledge, sometimes in a dense way. Graphic illustrations are helpful to readers but also require interpretation.

Behaviors to Notice and Support

	Student's Name						
Sustains attention over longer texts with more abstract, mature, and complex themes							
Notices, understands, and discusses a wide range of literary devices, such as flashbacks and stories within stories							
Deals with mature themes, such as family relationships, death, social injustice, and the supernatural							
Appreciates, understands, and discusses irony and satire							
Uses descriptive text as a way to understand settings and their importance to the plot or character development							
Discusses the setting as an element of the text, deciding whether it is important or unimportant							
Flexibly and automatically uses tools such as glossary, references, index, credentials for authors, legends, charts, and diagrams							
Notices aspects of the author's craft, including the way characters are described and presented as "real"							
Talks about the text in an analytic way, including finding specific evidence of the author's style							
Understands and is able to use the sophisticated, scholarly, and technical language that is found in informational texts							

USING THE
GUIDED READING PROGRAM

Characteristics of Text

Books categorized as Level Y present subtle themes and complex plots. As with earlier levels, they include a whole range of social problems as themes, but more explicit details (for example, about death or prejudice) may be provided. Readers will need to bring considerable world experience and reading experience to their understanding of these more mature texts. Writers use symbolism, irony, satire, and other literary devices that require readers to think beyond the literal meaning of the text.

Books at Level Y include many more complex works of fantasy that depict hero figures and heroic journeys. Readers are required to discern underlying lessons and also to analyze texts for traditional elements. Informational texts explore an ever-widening world of history and science; topics require extensive prior knowledge of complex concepts, as well as vocabulary. Readers are required to gather new information from reading and synthesize it with their current knowledge. A wide range of critical reading skills are also required, so that students continuously evaluate the quality and objectivity of the texts they read.

Behaviors to Notice and Support

Student's Name							
Understands and discusses subtle and complex plots and themes							
Understands, discusses, and deals in a mature way with a wide range of social problems, including social injustice and tragedy							
Understands and discusses in a mature way texts that present explicit details of social problems							
Understands literary irony and satire as they are used to communicate big ideas							
Understands complex fantasy, entering into whole new worlds, and understands concepts in relation to the imagined setting							
Understands and discusses the fact that words can have multiple meanings in relation to the context in which they are used							
Flexibly and automatically uses tools such as glossary, references, index, credentials for authors, legends, charts, and diagrams							
Interprets events in light of the setting—time, place, and culture							
Engages in critical thinking about fiction and nonfiction texts							
Critically evaluates nonfiction texts for accuracy and presentation of information							

USING THE
GUIDED READING PROGRAM

Characteristics of Text

Level Z captures books that require reading strategies similar to those needed at lower levels, but which present such mature themes that readers simply need more experience to deal with them. Some students who are widely read may need this challenge. Some informational books present complex and technical information, sometimes within a denser text. Others deal with controversial social concepts and political issues that require readers to evaluate several points of view. Critical reading is essential, and readers often have to reevaluate and revise their own previously held beliefs. Historical texts have detailed accounts of periods of history that are less well known. Readers learn new ways of finding technical information, and encounter complex examples of the basic organizational structures for informational texts. Fiction texts explore a wide range of human themes, often with graphic details of hardship, violence, or tragedy. High fantasy presents heroic quests, symbolism, and complex characters, and involves the reader in considering the meaning of life.

Behaviors to Notice and Support

Student's Name							
Sustains reading and understanding over much longer texts							
Deals with a great range of texts—from diaries to narratives to plays							
Switches easily from one genre to another, accessing knowledge of the structure and nature of the text while beginning to read							
Understands and discusses how a text "works" in terms of the writer's organization							
Deals with controversial social and political issues, seeing multiple perspectives							
Uses reading to gain technical knowledge in a wide variety of areas							
Understands the symbolism in heroic quests; applies concepts encountered in fantasy to today's life							
Flexibly and automatically uses tools such as glossary, references, index, credentials for authors, legends, charts, and diagrams							
Deals with and discusses in a mature way graphic details such as accounts of brutality, hardship, or violence							
Notices, understands, appreciates, and discusses literary devices							
Understands and appreciates complex language, archaic language, and cultural motifs							
Learns about epilogues, bibliographies, and forewords							
Builds information across the text, even when very unusual formats are used (for example, brief interviews with many characters)							
Fully understands the subtle differences between fiction and nonfiction							

READING LOG

	Child's Name								
LEVEL A									
Boxes									
Helping									
Hop, Skip, and Jump									
Little Animals									
My Dog Fluffy									
My House									
Playing									
Run, Rabbit!									
Storm, The									
Time									
LEVEL B									
Ants Go Home, The									
Fishing									
Getting There									
Home Run!									
Let's Play									
Look at Us									
My Feet									
Night Shift									
Off to the City									
Zebras Don't Brush Their Teeth!									
LEVEL C									
Big Blue Sea, The									
Brave Dave and the Dragons									
Hide and Seek									
It's Time to Eat!									
Little Blue Fish									
Little Duckling Is Lost									
Oak Street Party, The									
One Frog, One Fly									
Pass the Pasta, Please!									
Patterns									

READING LOG

Child's Name

LEVEL D

After School Fun								
Dog Walker, The								
Little Red Hen, The								
Little Turtle, The								
Noisy Breakfast, The								
Rainy Day, A								
Wake Up, Wake Up!								
What Do You See?								
Where in the World?								
Who Lives Here?								

LEVEL E

Flap and Sing: Birds								
Fred's Wish for Fish								
Fresh Fall Leaves								
I Go With Grandpa								
Let's Play Soccer								
Living Things								
Magic Pot, The								
No Snacks, Jack!								
Painting								
Yard Sale, The								

LEVEL F

Biscuit Visits the Big City								
Bug, a Bear, and a Boy, A								
Country Mouse and the Town Mouse, The								
Go Home, Daisy								
Goldilocks and the Three Bears								
How Lizard Lost His Colors								
Loose Tooth								
Meg and the Lost Pencil Case								
Melt It, Shape It: Glass								
Todd's Teacher								

GUIDED READING Fiction Focus, 2nd Edition

READING LOG

Child's Name

LEVEL G

At the Apple Farm								
Deep Blue Sea, The								
Gingerbread Man, The								
I Just Forgot								
In Our Yard								
Is This a Moose?								
Justin's New Bike								
Rabbit's Party								
Three Billy Goats Gruff, The								
Very Silly School, A								

LEVEL H

Aunt Maud's Mittens								
Father Who Walked on His Hands, The								
Good Morning, Monday								
Hop! Spring! Leap!								
Little Red Riding Hood								
Sammy the Seal								
Sione's Talo								
Trains								
Unusual Show, An								
Why Did the Chicken Cross the Road?								

LEVEL I

Animals at Night								
Dolphins and Porpoises								
Fat Cat, The: A Danish Folktale								
Mama Zooms								
Nana's Place								
Shoo, Fly Guy!								
Two Crazy Pigs								
Wax Man, The								
We're Going on a Nature Hunt								
Wheels on the Race Car, The								

READING LOG

Child's Name

LEVEL J

Title								
Antonio's Music								
Big, Brown Pot, The								
Big Cats								
Big Smelly Bear								
In the Barrio								
Just Us Women								
Kenny and the Little Kickers								
Poppleton Has Fun								
Safety in Numbers								
Young Cam Jansen and the Spotted Cat Mystery								

LEVEL K

Title								
Allie's Basketball Dream								
Andy Shane and the Very Bossy Dolores Starbuckle								
Don't Let the Pigeon Stay Up Late!								
Frog Prince, The								
Great Gracie Chase, The: Stop That Dog!								
Gym Teacher from the Black Lagoon, The								
Ibis: A True Whale Story								
Johnny Appleseed								
On My Way to Buy Eggs								
Three Days on a River in a Red Canoe								

LEVEL L

Title								
Alligator Baby								
Amelia Bedelia Under Construction								
Anansi the Spider: A Tale from the Ashanti								
Cam Jansen and the Secret Service Mystery								
Miss Nelson Has a Field Day								
Picking Apples & Pumpkins								
Ricky Ricotta's Mighty Robot vs. the Mecha-Monkeys From Mars								
Triple Rotten Day, The								
Worst Day of My Life, The								
Young Thurgood Marshall: Fighter for Equality								

READING LOG

Child's Name

LEVEL M

Alexander, Who's Not (Do you hear me? I mean it!) Going to Move								
Case of the Food Fight, The								
Dancing With the Indians								
How a House Is Built								
Ivy + Bean and the Ghost That Had to Go								
New Coat for Anna, A								
Penguin and the Pea, The								
Stink: The Incredible Shrinking Kid								
Stuart Goes to School								
Vampires Don't Wear Polka Dots (Bailey School Kids)								

LEVEL N

Alfie the Apostrophe								
Comic Guy: Our Crazy Class Election								
Fables								
Franny K. Stein, Mad Scientist: Frantastic Voyage								
Lion Dancer: Ernie Wan's Chinese New Year								
Mice and Beans								
Spy in the White House, A								
Suitcase								
Wonderful Alexander and the Catwings								
Zen Shorts								

LEVEL O

Amber Brown Is Green With Envy								
Angel Child, Dragon Child								
Can You Fly High, Wright Brothers?								
Chocolate Fever								
Jake Drake, Know-It-All								
Lost Treasure of the Emerald Eye								
Patchwork Quilt, The								
Pinduli								
Shark Lady: The Adventure of Eugenie Clark								
Talented Clementine, The								

READING LOG

Child's Name

LEVEL P

Countdown to the Year 1000								
Da Wild, Da Crazy, Da Vinci								
Helen Keller's Teacher								
Koya DeLaney and the Good Girl Blues								
Magic School Bus and the Science Fair Expedition, The								
Mariposa, La								
Nina, the Pinta, and the Vanishing Treasure, The (Alec Flint, Super Sleuth)								
Talking Eggs, The								
Who Stole The Wizard of Oz?								
You Can't See Your Bones with Binoculars, A Guide to Your 206 Bones								

LEVEL Q

Abby Takes a Stand								
Amulet: Book One, The Stonekeeper								
Bunnicula: A Rabbit-Tale of Mystery								
Champ								
Just Juice								
Life and Times of the Peanut, The								
Mummies, Pyramids, and Pharaohs: A Book About Ancient Egypt								
Oggie Cooder								
Punished!								
You Be the Detective								

LEVEL R

Achoo! The Most Interesting Book You'll Ever Read About Germs								
Island, The								
Julian Rodriguez Episode One: Trash Crisis on Earth								
More Than Anything Else								
Pocahontas and the Strangers								
Report Card, The								
Rules								
Trumpet of the Swan, The								
Wackiest White House Pets								
When Marian Sang								

READING LOG

Child's Name

LEVEL S

4 Kids in 5E & 1 Crazy Year							
Beethoven Lives Upstairs							
Bluish							
Dog's Life, A: The Autobiography of a Stray							
Granny Torrelli Makes Soup							
In the Shade of the Níspero Tree							
Let It Begin Here! Lexington & Concord: First Battles of the American Revolution							
Million Dollar Shot, The							
Puppies, Dogs, and Blue Northers							
Tru Confessions							

LEVEL T

10 Deadliest Plants, The							
Amazing Life of Benjamin Franklin, The							
Chasing Vermeer							
Dirty Tricks (Raven Hill Mysteries #5)							
Drita, My Homegirl							
Fair Weather							
Orphan Train Rider: One Boy's True Story							
Power of Un, The							
Replay							
Something Upstairs							

LEVEL U

Adventures of Marco Polo, The							
All of the Above							
Charlie Bone and the Invisible Boy							
Creepy Creatures (Goosebumps Graphix)							
Ginger Pie							
Graduation of Jake Moon, The							
Hush							
Nothing But the Truth: A Documentary Novel							
Tale of Despereaux, The							
Tangerine							

GUIDED READING Fiction Focus, 2nd Edition

READING LOG

Child's Name

LEVEL V

10 Most Wondrous Ancient Sites, The								
Becoming Naomi León								
Birdwing								
Desperate Journey								
Ellis Island								
Fall of the Amazing Zalindas, The: Sherlock Holmes and the Baker Street Irregulars								
Firework-Maker's Daughter, The								
Forty Acres and Maybe a Mule								
Foster's War								
Pictures of Hollis Woods								

LEVEL W

Blood on the River: James Town 1607								
Chu Ju's House								
Guilty By a Hair!								
Harriet Tubman, Secret Agent								
Home of the Brave								
Invention of Hugo Cabret, The								
Lightning Thief, The								
Lights, Camera, Amalee								
Out from Boneville (Bone)								
Tunnels								

LEVEL X

Antarctica								
Break With Charity, A: A Story About the Salem Witch Trials								
Fight for Freedom: The American Revolutionary War								
Four Pictures by Emily Carr								
Girl Named Disaster, A								
Millicent Min, Girl Genius								
Somewhere in the Darkness								
Storm Thief								
Usborne Book of Scientists, The: From Archimedes to Einstein								
When Hitler Stole Pink Rabbit								

READING LOG

	Child's Name								
LEVEL Y									
Artemis Fowl (Book 1)									
Boy Who Dared, The									
Geronimo									
Get On Out of Here, Philip Hall									
Heroes of the Holocaust									
Jumping Tree, The									
Larklight									
Pemba's Song: A Ghost Story									
Vlad the Impaler: The Real Count Dracula									
Yearling, The									
LEVEL Z									
An American Plague									
Best Ghost Stories Ever, The									
Detective Stories									
Finding My Hat									
Harry Potter and the Deathly Hallows									
Jane Eyre									
Malcolm X: By Any Means Necessary									
Stormbreaker: The First Alex Rider Adventure									
Time Machine, The									
Toning the Sweep									

EVALUATION RESPONSE FOR TEXT GRADIENT

adapted from *Guided Reading: Good First Teaching for All Children* (Fountas and Pinnell, 1996)

Directions: Since any gradient is always in the process of construction when it is used with varying groups of students, we expect our list to change every year. We encourage you to try the levels with your students and to provide feedback based on your own experiences. Please suggest changes to existing book levels and suggest new books for the list. Please provide the information requested.

Name: _____ **Grade Level You Teach:** _____

Telephone: _____ **E-mail Address:** _____

Address: _____

Book Evaluated

Book Title: _____ **Level:** _____

Author: _____ **Publisher:** _____

This book is

_____ A book that I have evaluated by using it with my class.

To what level should it be moved? _____

Why? _____

_____

_____ A book that I am recommending as a benchmark book.

How does it support readers at this level? _____

What challenge does it offer? _____

_____

_____ A new book that I am recommending to the collection.

At what level should it be placed? _____

Why? _____

_____

Copy and mail this form to:
Irene C. Fountas
Lesley University
Suite 2-029
1815 Massachusetts Avenue
Cambridge, MA 02140

ADDITIONAL LEVELED BOOKS AVAILABLE FROM SCHOLASTIC

Level A

I Am
by Adria Klein

My Cats
by Eileen Robinson

School Day!
by Jesus Cervantes

I See Bugs
by Wiley Blevins

We Are Painting
by Francie Alexander

What Do Insects Do?
by Susan Canizares

Level B

Dogs
by Amy Levin

Hats Around the World
by Liza Charlesworth

How Many Fish?
by Gosset & Ballinger

Lunch at the Zoo
by Wendy Blaxland

Monkeys
by Susan Canizares and Pamela Chanko

We Like Fruit
by Millen Lee

Level C

Bo and Peter
by Betsy Franco

In the City
by Susana Pasternac

Little Sister
by Robin Mitchell

Raindrops
by Sandy Gay

Swing, Swing, Swing
by Gail Tuchman

What Has Stripes?
by Margaret Ballinger

Level D

Don't Be Late!
by Akimi Gibson

The Haircut
by Armstrong & Hartley

I Love Mud and Mud Loves Me
by Vicki Stephens

I'm Hungry
by Judy Tuer

Hide and Seek
by Roberta Brown and Sue Carey

Making a Memory
by Margaret Ballinger

Level E

The Ball Game
by David Packard

Collections
by Margaret Ballinger and Rachel Gosset

A Funny Man
by Patricia Jensen

Just a Seed
by Wendy Blaxland

Paper Bag Trail
by Anne Schreiber

Tortillas
by Margarita González-Jensen

A Tree Can Be . . .
by Judy Nayer

Level F

Bread, Bread, Bread
by Ann Morris

How Far Will I Fly?
by Sachi Oyama

Itchy, Itchy Chicken Pox
by Grace Maccarone

My Dog's the Best
by Stephanie Calmenson

Shoveling Snow
by Pat Cummings

Who Stole the Cookies?
by Judith Moffat

"What Is That?" Said the Cat
by Grace Maccarone

Level G

All About You
by Catherine and Laurence Anholt

Buzz Said the Bee
by Wendy Cheyette Lewison

How Have I Grown?
by Mary Reid

I Shop with My Daddy
by Grace Maccarone

My Friends
by Taro Gomi

Say It, Sign It
by Elaine Epstein

Level H

A Clean House for Mole and Mouse
by Harriet Ziefert

I Was Walking Down the Road
by Sarah Barchas

Mr. McCready's Cleaning Day
by Tracey Shilling

The New Baby Calf
  by Edith Newlin Chase

Mom's Secret
  by Meredith Costain

Robert and the Rocket
  by Leesa Waldron

Level I

The Blue Mittens
  by Rachel Mann

Did You See Chip?
  by Wong Herbert Yee

Henny Penny
  by H. Werner Zimmermann

The Little Mouse, The Strawberry, and the Big Hungry Bear
  by Don & Audrey Wood

Look-Alike Animals
  by Robin Bernard

This Is the Place for Me
  by Joanna Cole

Level J

Bear's Bargain
  by Frank Asch

Big Mama and Grandma Ghana
  by Angela Shelf Medearis

Clifford the Big Red Dog
  by Norman Bridwell

Insects
  by Carolyn MacLulich

Mouse Soup
  by Arnold Lobel

Mr. Putter and Tabby Walk the Dog
  by Cynthia Rylant

My Father
  by Laura Mayer

Level K

Amalia and the Grasshopper
  by Jerry Tello

Bedtime for Frances
  by Russell Hoban

The Blind Men and the Elephant
  by Karen Backstein

The Bremen-Town Musicians
  by Ruth Belov Gross

Frog and Toad Are Friends
  by Arnold Lobel

Harry and Willy and Carrothead
  by Judith Caseley

Keep the Lights Burning, Abbie
  by Peter & Connie Roop

Level L

Alexander and the Wind-Up Mouse
  by Leo Lionni

Black Bear Cub
  by Alan Lind

Happy Birthday, Martin Luther King
  by Jean Marzollo

Horrible Harry and the Ant Invasion
  by Suzy Kline

Katy and the Big Snow
  by Virginia Lee Barton

The Schoolyard Mystery: Invisible Inc. #1
  by Elizabeth Levy

Teach Us, Amelia Bedelia
  by Peggy Parish

Level M

Boundless Grace
  by Mary Hoffman

Cloudy With a Chance of Meatballs
  by Judi Barrett

Five True Dog Stories
  by Margaret Davidson

George Washington's Mother
  by Jean Fritz

Ghost Versus Ghost: BBS #8
  by Jan & Stan Berenstain

Mummies in the Morning (Magic Tree House #3)
  by Mary Pope Osborne

Level N

The Cat Who Wore a Pot on Her Head
  by Jan Slepian & Ann Seidler

Chicken Sunday
  by Patricia Polacco

Desert Life
  by Rachel Mann

Doctor DeSoto
  by William Steig

The Popcorn Book
  by Tomie dePaola

Tikki Tikki Tembo
  by Arlene Mosel

Level O

The Boxcar Children #1
  by Gertrude Warner Chandler

The Cat's Meow
  by Gary Soto

Class Clown
  by Johanna Hurwitz

ADDITIONAL LEVELED BOOKS AVAILABLE FROM SCHOLASTIC

The Legend of the Bluebonnet
by Tomie dePaola

Owl Moon
by Jane Yolen

The Secret Soldier
by Ann McGovern

The Story of Ruby Bridges
by Robert Coles

Level P

The Adventures of Captain Underpants
by Dav Pilkey

Encyclopedia Brown Takes the Cake!
by Donald J. Sobol

It's Mine!
by Leo Lionni

Kid Power
by Susan Beth Pfeffer

The Pagemaster
by Jordan Horowitz

Wanted Dead or Alive: The True Story of Harriet Tubman
by Ann McGovern

Level Q

Great Black Heroes: Five Brave Explorers
by Wade Hudson

Knitwits
by William Taylor

Mr. Popper's Penguins
by Richard and Florence Atwater

Sarah Morton's Day
by Kate Waters

The True Story of the 3 Little Pigs
by Jon Scieszka

We'll Never Forget You, Roberto Clemente
by Trudie Engel

Level R

Gentle Annie
by Mary Francis Shura

The Great Kapok Tree
by Lynne Cherry

Misty of Chincoteague
by Marguerite Henry

Phoebe the Spy
by Judith Berry Griffin

Run Away Home
by Patricia C. McKissack

They Came From Center Field
by Dan Gutman

Level S

Afternoon of the Elves
by Janet Taylor Lisle

Lon Po Po
by Ed Young

Samuel's Choice
by Richard Berleth

Sixth Grade Secrets
by Louis Sachar

The Story of the White House
by Kate Waters

The Young Man and the Sea
by Rodman Philbrick

Level T

Bridge to Terabithia
by Katherine Paterson

Fur, Feathers, and Flippers
by Patricia Lauber

Freedom Train
by Dorothy Sterling

A Light in the Storm
by Karen Hesse

Surviving the Applewhites
by Stephanie S. Tolan

Level U

Bad, Badder, Baddest
by Cynthia Voigt

Ella Enchanted
by Gail Carson Levine

The Journal of Jedediah Barstow: An Emigrant on the Oregon Trail
by Ellen Levine

Number the Stars
by Lois Lowry

P.S. Long Letter Later
by Paula Danziger and Ann M. Martin

Report to the Principal's Office
by Jerry Spinelli

Level V

The Golden Goblet
by Eloise Jarvis McGraw

A Long Way from Chicago
by Richard Peck

SOS Titanic
by Eve Bunting

The Thief Lord
by Cornelia Funke

The Secret of NIMH
by Robert C. O'Brien

Watchers #6: Lab 6
by Peter Lerangis

Level W

The Great Fire
by Jim Murphy

**John and Abigail Adams:
An American Love Story**
by Judith St. George

Maniac Magee
by Jerry Spinelli

Max the Mighty
by Rodman Philbrick

**Song Quest
(The Echorium Sequence)**
by Katherine Roberts

Walk Two Moons
by Sharon Creech

Level X

**13 Ghosts: Strange but True
Stories**
by Will Osborne

Bone Dance
by Martha Brooks

**Childtimes: a Three-Generation
Memoir**
by Eloise Greenfield and
Lessie Jones Little

Cowboys of the Wild West
by Russell Freedman

The Iceberg Hermit
by Arthur Roth

Pyramid
by David Macaulay

**Zlata's Diary: A Child's Life in
Sarajevo**
by Zlata Filipovic

Level Y

Bull Run
by Paul Fleischman

The Call of the Wild
by Jack London, with an
introduction by Avi

Confucius: The Golden Rule
by Russell Freedman

The Ear, the Eye, and the Arm
by Nancy Farmer

Losing Joe's Place
by Gordon Korman

**Now Is Your Time! The African-
American Struggle for Freedom**
by Walter Dean Myers

Numbering All the Bones
by Ann Rinaldi

Level Z

Anne Frank: In the World
compiled by the
Anne Frank House

**The Journal of Patrick Seamus
Flaherty: United States Marine
Corps, Khe Sanh, Vietnam, 1968**
by Ellen Emerson White

**Louis Armstrong: Singing,
Swinging, Satchmo**
by Sanford Brown

**Memories of Vietnam: War in the
First Person**
by Ellen Weiss

The Raven and Other Poems
by Edgar Allan Poe

**Red Scarf Girl: A Memoir of a
Cultural Revolution**
by Ji-li Jiang

Samir and Yonatan
by Daniella Carmi

Related Books Chart

Level	Guided Reading Fiction Focus — Title	Titles Related By: Genre/Author/Series	Titles Related By: Theme/Topic
A	Boxes	1, 2, 3 in the Box by Ellen Tarlow GRB	
A	Helping	We Are Painting by Francie Alexander	
A	Hop, Skip, and Jump	Games by Samantha Berger GRC	
A	Little Animals	Legs by Rachel Ballinger GRB	
A	My Dog Fluffy	Dogs by Amy Levin GRB	
A	My House	We Read by Wiley Blevins	We Live Here by Gabriel Salzman GRB
A	Playing		We Play Together by Wiley Blevins GRA
A	Run, Rabbit!	What Bears Like by Janelle Cherrington GRA	
A	Storm, The	What's the Weather? by Jennifer Calii GRB	
A	Time	School Day! by Jesus Cervantes GRA	
B	Ants Go Home, The		How Many Ants? Rookie Reader GRE
B	Fishing	In the Woods by Akimi Gibson GRB	
B	Getting There		Let's Go GRA
B	Home Run!		The Ball Game by David Packard GRD
B	Let's Play	Who Hid? by Nancy Leber GRB	
B	Look At Us		Fun With Simple Machines by Ellen Tarlow GRC
B	My Feet	Who Am I? by Millen Lee GRD	
B	Night Shift	At Work by Ellen Geist GRC	
B	Off to the City	How to Make a Wind Sock by Ellen Tarlow GRB	
B	Zebras Don't Brush Their Teeth!	Monkeys by Susan Canizares	What Has Stripes? by Margaret Ballinger GRB
C	Big Blue Sea, The		I See Fish by Don L. Curry GRB
C	Brave Dave and the Dragons	Giants by Wendy Blaxland GRF	
C	Hide and Seek	Swing, Swing, Swing by Gail Tuchman	
C	It's Time to Eat!		What's for Lunch? by Eric Carle GRC

Level	Guided Reading Fiction Focus — Title	Titles Related By: Genre/Author/Series	Titles Related By: Theme/Topic
C	Little Blue Fish	How Many Fish? by Rachel Gosset and Margaret Ballinger GRB	
C	Little Duckling Is Lost	In the Forest by Melissa Schiller GRC	
C	Oak Street Party, The	Lunch at the Zoo by Wendy Blaxland and C. Brimage GRB	
C	One Frog, One Fly		Frog's Lunch by Dee Lillegard GRE
C	Pass the Pasta, Please!		In the Kitchen by Susan Canizares and Betsey Chassen
C	Patterns		Look and Find Shapes by Wiley Blevins GRB
D	After School Fun	The Tree House by Robert Brown and Sue Carey GRE	
D	Dog Walker, The	My Dog Talks by Gail Herman GRE	
D	Little Red Hen, The	Goldilocks by Ellen Tarlow GRC	
D	Little Turtle, The		What Is That? Said the Cat by Grace Maccarone
D	Noisy Breakfast, The		My Best Sandwich by Susan Hartley and Shane Armstrong; I'm Hungry by Judy Tuer GRD
D	Rainy Day, A		Clouds by Meredith Costain
D	Wake Up, Wake Up!		What Time Is It? by Julie Moriarty GRD
D	What Do You See?	Look, Listen, and Learn by Susan Canizares and Pamela Chanko GRE	
D	Where in the World?		You Say Hola, I Say Hello by Elizabeth Zapata GRD
D	Who Lives Here?	Animal Pals by Janelle Cherrington GRE	
E	Flap and Sing: Birds	Series: Investigators: Life Cycles	Animal Babies by Bobbie Hamsa GRE; A Chick Grows Up by Pam Zollman GRG; Parrots and Other Birds by Mary Shulte GRG
E	Fred's Wish for Fish	I Shop with My Daddy by Grace Maccarone GRG	
E	Fresh Fall Leaves		A Tree Can Be . . . by Judy Nayer GRE
E	I Go with Grandpa	Let's Go to a Museum by Wiley Blevins GRB	Going to Grandma's Farm Rookie Reader GRC
E	Let's Play Soccer	I Know Karate by Mary Packard GRE	
E	Living Things	Series: Farm Animals GRE, F (12 books); Series: The World of Insects GRG (22 books)	
E	Magic Pot, The	Monkey See, Monkey Do by Marc Gave GRE	

* One title in a series

Level	Title	Genre/Author/Series	Theme/Topic
E	No Snacks, Jack!		Eat Your Peas, Louise! by Pegeen Snow GRE
E	Painting		Harry's House by Angela Shelf Medearis GRF
E	Yard Sale, The		Markets by Pamela Chenko and Samantha Berger GRD
F	Biscuit Visits the Big City		Tina's Taxi by Betsy Franco GRF
F	Bug, a Bear, and a Boy, A	Read to Your Bunny by Rosemary Wells GRF	
F	Go Home, Daisy	Biscuit Visits the Big City by Alyssa Satin Capucilli GRF	
F	How Lizard Lost His Colors	Troll Tricks Phonics Reader GRH	
F	Loose Tooth	Itchy, Itchy Chicken Pox by Grace Maccarone GRF	
F	Meg and the Lost Pencil Case	The 100th Day by Grace Maccarone GRG	
F	Melt It, Shape It: Glass	Series: Investigators: Materials	Solids, Liquids, and Glass by Ginger Garrett GRG
F	Todd's Teacher	My Dog's the Best by Stephanie Calmenson GRF	
G	At the Apple Farm	We Love Fruit by Allan Fowler GRH	
G	Deep Blue Sea, The	Alphabet Mystery by Audrey Wood* GRI	Apples to Applesauce by Inez Snyder GRE
G	Gingerbread Man, The		The Gingerbread Man by Rita Rose GRI
G	I Just Forgot	More Spaghetti, I Say! by Rita Gelman GRG	
G	In Our Yard	Maple Trees by Allan Fowler GRH	Log Hotel by Ann Schreiber GRI
G	Is This a Moose?	It Could Still Be a Mammal GRH	
G	Justin's New Bike	Soccer Game! by Grace Maccarone GRF	
G	Rabbit's Party	My Friends by Taro Gomi GRG	
G	Three Billy Goats Gruff, The	Henny Penny by Werner H. Zimmermann GRI	
G	Very Silly School, A	A Dog for Each Day Rookie Reader GRG; Addition Annie Rookie Reader GRG; Willie's Wonderful Pet by Mel Cebulash GRI	
H	Aunt Maud's Mittens	Jenny's Socks Rookie Reader GRG	
H	Father Who Walked on His Hands, The		The Voyage of Mae Jemison by Susan Canizares GRH; A Day With Firefighters Welcome Book, GRH
H	Good Morning, Monday	City Sounds by Jean Marzollo GRG	
H	Hop! Spring! Leap!		Look-Alike Animals by Robin Bernard GRH
H	Sammy the Seal	Rapid Robert Roadrunner by Bob Reese GRF	
H	Sione's Talo	The Very Big Potato by Janelle Cherrington GRA	

Level	Title	Genre/Author/Series	Theme/Topic
H	Trains	Energy and Motion by Melissa Stewart GRI	What Is a Wheel and Axle? by Lloyd G. Douglas GRF
H	Unusual Show, An	Birds on Stage by Saturnino Romay GRH	
H	Why Did the Chicken Cross the Road?	The Dinosaur Who Lived in My Backyard by Brendan G. Hennessy GRI	
I	Animals at Night	Snap! A Book About Alligators and Crocodiles by M. and G. Berger* GRK	
I	Dolphins and Porpoises		Friendly Dolphins by Allan Fowler GRH
I	Mama Zooms		Say It, Sign It by Elaine Epstein GRG
I	Nana's Place	Going to Grandma's by John Tarlton GRI	Big Mama and Grandma Ghana by Angela Shelf Medearis GRJ
I	Shoo, Fly Guy!	Hi, Fly Guy! by Tedd Arnold* GRI	
I	Two Crazy Pigs	The Dumb Bunnies by Dav Pilkey GRJ	
I	Wax Man, The	The Boy Who Cried Wolf by Freya Littledale GRJ	
I	We're Going on a Nature Hunt	Apples and Pumpkins by Ann Rockwell GRI	
I	Wheels on the Race Car, The	The Big Hungry Bear by Don & Audrey Wood GRI	
J	Antonio's Music	Nana's Fiddle by Larry Dane Brimner GRI	
J	Big Cats	Series: True Books: Animals That Hunt; Series: Investigators: Predators	Your Pet Cat by Elaine Landau GRL
J	Big Smelly Bear	Wake Me in Spring by James Preller GRJ	
J	Big, Brown Pot, The	Who Took the Farmer's Hat? By Joan Nodset GRI	
J	In the Barrio	We Scream for Ice Cream by Bernice Chardiet GRK	
J	Just Us Women	A Day With the Family by David Parker GRJ	
J	Kenny and the Little Kickers	Froggy Learns to Swim by Jonathan London GRJ	
J	Poppleton Has Fun	Series: Poppleton by Cynthia Rylant*	
J	Safety in Numbers	Series: Investigators: Survival	
J	Young Cam Jansen and the Spotted Cat Mystery	Series: Cam Jansen by David Adler	
K	Allie's Basketball Dream		Amazing Grace by Mary Hoffman GRL
K	Andy Shane and the Very Bossy Dolores Starbuckle	Officer Buckle and Gloria by Peggy Rathman GRL	
K	Don't Let the Pigeon Stay Up Late!	Don't Let the Pigeon Drive the Bus by Mo Willems GRL	
K	Frog Prince, The	The Blind Men and the Elephant by Karen Backstein GRK	
K	Great Gracie Chase, The: Stop That Dog!	Henry and Mudge and the Sneaky Crackers by Cynthia Rylant* GRJ	

* One title in a series

Level	Title	Genre/Author/Series	Theme/Topic
K	Gym Teacher from the Black Lagoon, The	Series: The Black Lagoon by Mike Thaler	
K	Ibis: A True Whale Story		Beluga Whales by Ann O. Squire GRL
K	Johnny Appleseed		When I First Came to This Land by Harriet Ziefert GRK
K	On My Way to Buy Eggs	Josephine's Imagination by Arnold Dobrin GRL	
K	Three Days on a River in a Red Canoe		The Amazon River by Mary Schulte GRJ; The Colorado River by Dale-Marie Bryan GRJ; The Mississippi River by Allan Fowler GRJ; The Missouri River by Christine Taylor-Butler GRJ; The Nile River by Allan Fowler GRI
L	Alligator Baby	Alexander and the Windup Mouse by Leo Lionni GRL	
L	Amelia Bedelia Under Construction	Series: Amelia Bedelia by Peggy Parish GRL	
L	Anansi the Spider: A Tale from the Ashanti	Little One Inch by Akimi Gibson GRK	
L	Cam Jansen and the Secret Service Mystery	The Schoolyard Mystery by Elizabeth Levy GRL	
L	Miss Nelson Has a Field Day	Series: Miss Nelson by Harry Allard GRL	
L	Picking Apples & Pumpkins	Series: Food and Nutrition: Apples, Bananas	
L	Ricky Ricotta's Mighty Robot vs. the Mecha-Monkeys From Mars	A Day in Space by Suzanne Lord and Jolie Epstein GRL	
L	Triple Rotten Day, The	Tooth Trouble by Abby Klein GRL	
L	Worst Day of My Life, The	Series: Little Bill by Bill Cosby* GRL	
L	Young Thurgood Marshall: Fighter for Equality		Extraordinary People of the Civil Rights Movement by Sheila and P. Stephen Hardy GRN
M	Alexander, Who's Not (Do you hear me? I mean it!) Going to Move	Alexander and the Terrible, Horrible, No Good, Very Bad Day by Judith Viorst GRM	
M	Case of the Food Fight, The	Kids in Ms. Coleman's Class: Author Day by Ann M. Maartin GRL	
M	Dancing With the Indians		Little Hawk's New Name by Don Bolognose
M	How a House Is Built		Is This My House? by Arthur Dorros GRL
M	Ivy + Bean and the Ghost That Had to Go	The Berenstain Bear Scouts: The Ghost Versus Ghost by Jan and Stan Berenstain GRM	
M	New Coat for Anna, A	The Quilt Story by Tony Johnston and Tomie de Paola GRL	
M	Stink: The Incredible Shrinking Kid	Series: Stink by Megan McDonald	
M	Stuart Goes to School	Stuart's Cape by Sara Pennypacker*	
M	Vampires Don't Wear Polka Dots (Bailey School Kids)	Series: The Adventures of the Bailey School Kids	
N	Alfie the Apostrophe		Nouns and Verbs Have a Field Day by Robin Pulver GRT

Level	Title	Genre/Author/Series	Theme/Topic
N	Comic Guy: Our Crazy Class Election	School's Out by Joanna Hurwitz GRN	
N	Fables	The Tortoise Shell and Other African Stories by Geof Smith GRN	
N	Franny K. Stein, Mad Scientist: Frantastic Voyage	The Neighbor From Outer Space by Maureen George GRN	
N	Lion Dancer: Ernie Wan's Chinese New Year		China, True Book GRN; Fiesta! Festivals and Holidays GRM
N	Mice and Beans	Julius, The Baby of the World by Kevin Henkes GRN	
N	Spy in the White House, A	Series: Capital Mysteries by Ron Roy GRM	
N	Suitcase	Justin and the Best Biscuits in the World by Mildred Pitts Walter* GRP	
N	Wonderful Alexander and the Catwings	Catwings; Catwings Return by Ursula Le Guin GRN	
N	Zen Shorts	The Three Questions by Jon Muth* GRM	
O	Amber Brown Is Green With Envy	Series: Amber Brown by Paula Danziger GRN	
O	Angel Child, Dragon Child	Every Cloud Has a Silver Lining by Anne Mazer GRQ	
O	Can You Fly High, Wright Brothers?	How to Eat Fried Worms by Thomas Rockwell GRR	Amelia Earhart: Adventure in the Sky by Sara Pennypacker GRO
O	Chocolate Fever		
O	Jake Drake, Know-It-All	Series: Jake Drake by Andrew Clements GRM	
O	Lost Treasure of the Emerald Eye	The Hidden Stairs and the Magic Carpet by Tony Abbott GRO	
O	Patchwork Quilt, The	Grandma's Records by Eric Velasquez GRO	
O	Pinduli	Crickwing by Janell Cannon* GRO	
O	Shark Lady: True Adventures of Eugenie Clark	Series: Inventors and Scientists Children's Press	
O	Talented Clementine, The	Series: Clementine by Sara Pennypacker GRQ	
P	Alec Flint Super Sleuth: The Nina, The Pinta, and the Vanishing Treasure (Alec Flint Mystery #1)	The Secret, Secret Passage by A.E. Parker GRP	
P	Countdown to the Year 1000	Series: The Dragon Slayers' Academy by Kate McMullan	
P	Da Wild, Da Crazy, Da Vinci	The Time Warp Trio GRP	
P	Helen Keller's Teacher		Helen Keller by Margaret Davidson
P	Koya DeLaney and the Good Girl Blues	Kid Power by Susan Beth Pfeffer GRP	
P	Magic School Bus and the Science Fair Expedition, The	Series: Magic School Bus	
P	Mariposa, La	Oh, Brother by Wilson GRP	
P	Who Stole The Wizard of Oz?	The True Confessions of Charlotte Doyle* GRV	
P	You Can't See Your Bones with Binoculars, A Guide to Your 206 Bones	A Dinosaur Named Sue by Fay Robinson GRP	Bones by Seymour Simon GRX

* One title in a series

Level	Title	Genre/Author/Series	Theme/Topic
Q	Abby Takes a Stand	Run Away Home by Pat McKissack* GRR	
Q	Bunnicula: A Rabbit-Tale of Mystery	The Easter Bunny That Ate My Sister by Dave Marney GRQ	
Q	Champ	They Came From Center Field by Dan Gutman GRR	
Q	Just Juice	Music of the Dolphins by Karen Hesse* GRV	
Q	Life and Times of the Peanut, The	All About Seeds by Melvin Berger GRQ	
Q	Mummies, Pyramids, and Pharaohs: A Book About Ancient Egypt	The Aztec: A True Book GRQ	
Q	Oggie Cooder	Bunnies in the Bathroom by Ben Baglio GRQ	
Q	Punished!	Series: Help! I'm Trapped by Todd Strasser GRQ	
Q	You Be the Detective	Series: You Be the Detective by Marvin Mille GRQ	
R	Achoo! The Most Interesting Book You'll Ever Read About Germs	Calcium: A True Book GRQ	
R	Julian Rodriguez Episode One: Trash Crisis on Earth	Ghostmobile by Kathy Kennedy Tapp GRS	
R	More Than Anything Else	Freedom Crossing by Margaret Goff Clark GRR	
R	Pocahontas and the Strangers		If You Lived With the Cherokee; If You Lived With the Hopi; If You Sailed on the Mayflower GRQ
R	Report Card, The	There's a Tarantula in My Homework by Susan Clymer GRR	
R	Rules	No Talking by Andrew Clements GRR	
R	Trumpet of the Swan, The	Charlotte's Web; Stuart Little by E.B. White*	
R	Wackiest White House Pets	Series: Getting to Know the U.S. Presidents GRR	
R	When Marian Sang	Duke Ellington by Mike Venezia GRR	
S	4 Kids in 5E and 1 Crazy Year	Fifth Grade: Here Comes Trouble by Colleen O'Shaughnessy McKenna GRS	
S	Beethoven Lives Upstairs		George Handel by Mike Venezia GRR
S	Bluish: A Novel	Second Cousins by Virginia Hamilton* GRQ	
S	Dog's Life, A: The Autobiography of a Stray	Home for the Howl-idays by Diane Curtis Regan GRS	
S	Granny Torrelli Makes Soup		Salsa Stories by Lulu Delacre GRS
S	In the Shade of the Nispero Tree	The Star Fisher by Laurence Yep GRS	
S	Let It Begin Here! Lexington & Concord: First Battles of the American Revolution		Valley Forge by Richard Anmon GRS
S	Million Dollar Shot, The	The Million Dollar Putt by Gutman GRR	
S	Puppies, Dogs, and Blue Northers	War Dog Heroes: True Stories of Dog Courage in Wartime by Jeannette Sanderson GRS	

Level	Title	Genre/Author/Series	Theme/Topic
S	Tru Confessions	Good-Bye My Wishing Star by Vicki Gore GRS	
T	10 Deadliest Plants, The	Desert Giants: The World of the Saguaro Cactus GRR	
T	Amazing Life of Benjamin Franklin, The		Will You Sign Here, John Hancock?
T	Chasing Vermeer	The Wright 3; The Calder Game by Blue Balliett* GRV	
T	Dirty Tricks (Raven Hill Mysteries #5)	Series: Raven Hill Mysteries	
T	Drita My Homegirl	Cybil War by Betsy Byers GRS	
T	Fair Weather	A Year Down Under by Richard Peck GRV	
T	Orphan Train Rider: One Boy's True Story	Journey to Ellis Island: How My Father Came to America GRT	
T	Power of Un, The		The Werewolf Chronicles by Rodman Philbrick and Lynn Harnett GRT
T	Replay	The Wanderer by Sharon Creech* GRV	
T	Something Upstairs	The Secret Garden by Frances Burnett GRU	
U	Adventures of Marco Polo, The		Great Explorations by David Neufield GRT
U	All of the Above	Heaven by Angela Johnson GRU	
U	Charlie Bone and the Invisible Boy	Book of Monsters: Tales to Give You the Creeps by Bruce Coulie GRT	
U	Creepy Creatures (Goosebumps Graphix)	Ranger's Apprentice: The Ruins of Gorian by John Flanagan GRU	
U	Ginger Pye	The Girl in the Window by Wilma Yeo GRU	
U	Graduation of Jake Moon, The	Report to the Principal's Office by Jerry Spinelli GRU	
U	Hush	The Ashwater Experiment by Amy Goldman Koss GRU	
U	Nothing But the Truth: A Documentary Novel	Midnight Magic by Avi* GRU	
U	Tale of Despereaux, The	George Washington's Socks by Elvira Woodruff GRT	
U	Tangerine	Do The Funkie Pickle by Jerry Spinelli GRU	
V	10 Most Wondrous Ancient Sites, The	What a Great Ideal Inventions That Changed the World GRV	
V	Becoming Naomi León	Anne of Green Gables by L.M. Montgomery GRV	
V	Birdwing	Skeleton Man by Joseph Bruchac GRV	
V	Desperate Journey	The Hero of Ticonderoga by Gail Gauthia GRV	
V	Ellis Island	Series: Cornerstones of Freedom GRV	
V	Fall of the Amazing Zalindas, The: Sherlock Holmes and the Baker Street Irregulars	Scary Stories 3: More Tales to Chill Your Bones	
V	Firework-Maker's Daughter, The	Dustland by Virginia Hamilton GRV	

* One title in a series

Level	Title	Genre/Author/Series	Theme/Topic
V	Forty Acres and Maybe a Mule		Color Me Dark Dear America series GRV
V	Foster's War		Battle for Iwo Jima Cornerstones of Freedom Series GRW
V	Pictures of Hollis Woods		Esperanza Rising by Pam Muñoz Ryan GRV
W	Blood on the River: James Town 1607	Series: Cornerstones of Freedom GRW	The Jamestown Colony Cornerstones of Freedom Series GRV
W	Chu Ju's House		The Moon Bridge by Marcia Savin GRW
W	Guilty By a Hair!	Series: 24/7 :Science Behind the Scenes GRW	
W	Harriet Tubman: Secret Agent	Escape North: The Story of Harriet Tubman by Monica Kulling GRN	If You Traveled on the Underground Railroad by Ellen Levine GRQ; Get on Board: The Story of the Underground Railroad by Jim Haskins; Enemies of Slavery by David A. Adler GRT
W	Home of the Brave		Journey to a New World My America Series GRV; Where the River Runs: A Portrait of a Refugee Family by Nancy Price Graff GRW
W	Invention of Hugo Cabret, The	Mama, Let's Dance by Patricia Hermes GRW	
W	Lightning Thief, The	The Seventh Tower: The Fall of Garth Nix GRW	
W	Out From Boneville	Bone: The Dragonslayer by Jeff Smith GRW	
W	Tunnels (Book 1)	Inkheart by Cornelia Funke GRA	
X	Antarctica	The Glory Field by Walter Dean Myers* GRX	
X	Break With Charity, A: A Story About the Salem Witch Trials	Series: My Name Is America	
X	Fight for Freedom: The American Revolutionary War		Spies on the Devil's Belt by Betsy Hayes; John and Abigail Adams: An American Love Story by Judith St. George GRW
X	Four Pictures by Emily Carr	Extraordinary Women Journalists by Claire Price-Groff GRW	
X	Girl Named Disaster, A	Definitely Cool by Brenda Wilkinson GRX	
X	Millicent Min, Girl Genius	Moccasin Trail by Eloise McGraw	
X	Somewhere in the Darkness	At Her Majesty's Request: An African Princess in Victorian England by Walter Dean Myers* GRX	

Level	Title	Genre/Author/Series	Theme/Topic
X	Storm Thief, The	Point Blank by Anthony Horowitz GRX	
X	Usborne Book of Scientists, The: From Archimedes to Einstein	The Usborne Book of Inventors: From DaVinci to Biro	
X	When Hitler Stole Pink Rabbit	Sarah Bishop by Scott O'Dell GRX	
Y	Artemis Fowl (Book 1)	Series: Artemis Fowl	
Y	Boy Who Dared, The		Heroes of the Holocaust: True Stories of Rescues by Teens GRY
Y	Geronimo		The Forgotten Heroes: The Story of the Buffalo Soldiers by Clinton Cox GRX
Y	Get On Out of Here, Philip Hall	And Now Miguel by Joseph Krumgold GRZ	
Y	Heroes of the Holocaust		Memories of Anne Frank by Leslie Alison Gold GRX
Y	Jumping Tree, The	Jesse by Gary Soto	
Y	Larklight	Arthur: The Seeing Stone by Kevin Crossley-Holland GRY	
Y	Pemba's Song: A Ghost Story	13 Ghosts: Strange but True Stories by Will Osborne GRX	
Y	Vlad the Impaler: The Real Count Dracula	The Edge of the Sword by Rebecca Tingle GRX	
Y	Yearling, The	White Fang by Jack London GRX	
Z	An American Plague: The True and Terrifying Story of the Yellow Fever Epidemic		
Z	Best Ghost Stories Ever, The	Clockwork by Philip Pullman GRZ	
Z	Detective Stories	The Golden Goblet by Eloise Jarvis GRV	
Z	Finding My Hat		I Am an American: A True Story of Japanese Internment GRZ
Z	Harry Potter and the Deathly Hallows	Series: Harry Potter	
Z	Jane Eyre		Invincible Louisa by Cornelia Meiss GRZ
Z	Malcolm X: By Any Means Necessary	The Greatest: Muhammad Ali by Walter Dean Myers GRZ	
Z	Stormbreaker: The First Alex Rider Adventure	Series: Alex Rider by Anthony Horowitz	
Z	Time Machine, The	The Last Book in the Universe by Philbrick Rodman GRW	
Z	Toning the Sweep	Make Lemonade by Virginia Euwer Wolff GRZ	

* One title in a series

TECHNOLOGY

Information on Guided Reading and how to implement it in your classroom is provided at **www.scholastic.com.** In addition, the site contains numerous teacher, student, and parent resources related to books in the Guided Reading Program. Use these resources for independent and group extension activities.

teacher resources

student activities

Scholastic Reading Counts! quizzes are available for all the titles in the Guided Reading Program. These quizzes can be used to monitor student comprehension and make decisions about each student's instructional needs.

Dear Family Member:

Your child is becoming a skilled independent reader! And the guided reading books that your reader will bring home are designed to help in this process.

As part of the *Scholastic Guided Reading Program,* your child will participate in small groups and will receive individualized instruction to develop fluency, oral language, vocabulary, phonics, comprehension, and writing skills. In addition, your child will bring home enjoyable, level-appropriate stories and selections that will help to ensure his or her success as an independent reader.

Here are some suggestions for helping your child before, during, and after reading:

Before

- Look at the book cover with your child. Together, review the illustrations or photographs in the book. Ask your child to predict what the story or selection will be about.

- Discuss what you and your child might already know about the topic of the book you are about to read.

- If your child is a beginning reader, echo-read the story or selection with your child by reading a line first and having your child read it after you. If your child is a more skilled reader, periodically stop and ask questions.

During

- If your child does not recognize a word right away, help him or her to focus on the familiar letters and spelling patterns in the word. Guide your child to think about other words that look like the unfamiliar word.

- Encourage your child to use phonics and decoding skills to sound out any new, unfamiliar words. If necessary, provide the word if your child struggles.

- Encourage your child to read with expression and to enjoy reading!

After

- Encourage your child to reread the story or selection to develop confidence. If the book is long, reread a few favorite sections or chapters. Perhaps your child could read the story or selection to other family members or friends.

- Discuss the story or selection with your child. Ask questions such as: What were your favorite parts? Who were your favorite characters? Why? What interesting fact did you learn?

- Have your child keep a journal of favorite stories and selections and interesting words in those books. Your child might also like to write about the book in this journal.

Have fun with this reading experience and your child will have fun, too!

Sincerely,

Estimado padre o tutor:

Su niño está en el proceso de convertirse en un lector hábil e independiente. Los libros de lectura guiada que su niño llevará a casa han sido concebidos para ayudar en este proceso.

Como parte del Programa de Lectura Guiada de Scholastic, su niño recibirá instrucción en grupos pequeños e individualizada con el objetivo de desarrollar la fluidez, el lenguaje oral, el vocabulario, la fonética, la comprensión y las destrezas de escritura. Además, su niño llevará a casa lecturas amenas y apropiadas a su nivel, que le servirán para garantizar su éxito como lector independiente.

Éstas son algunas sugerencias para ayudar a su niño antes, durante y después de la lectura:

Antes

- Observe con su niño la cubierta del libro. Repasen juntos las ilustraciones o fotografías del libro. Pídale a su niño predecir de qué tratará el cuento o la selección que van a leer.

- Comenten lo que usted y su niño ya sepan sobre el tema del libro que van a leer.

- Si su niño es un lector principiante, lea usted primero una línea y pídale que lea esa misma línea después. Si su niño es un lector más avanzado, haga una pausa de vez en cuando para hacerle preguntas.

Durante

- Si a su niño le resulta difícil reconocer alguna palabra, ayúdelo a fijarse en las letras y patrones ortográficos con los que esté familiarizado. Guíe a su niño en la búsqueda de otras palabras que se parezcan a la palabra desconocida.

- Anime a su niño a usar la fonética y las destrezas de decodificación para leer en voz alta cualquier palabra nueva o desconocida. Si su niño tiene dificultades para hacerlo de manera independiente, lea usted la palabra.

- Anime a su niño a leer de manera expresiva y a disfrutar de la lectura.

Después

- Anime a su niño a volver a leer el cuento o la selección para que gane confianza como lector. Si el libro es demasiado largo, vuelva a leer algunas de las secciones o pasajes favoritos. También puede pedirle que lea el cuento a otros familiares o amigos.

- Comente con su niño el cuento o la selección. Hágale preguntas como las siguientes: ¿Qué partes te gustaron más? ¿Qué personajes son tus favoritos? ¿Por qué? ¿Qué hecho o dato importante aprendiste leyendo este libro?

- Pídale que lleve un récord de sus cuentos y selecciones favoritos, así como de las palabras interesantes que encuentre en los mismos. También, puede llevar un diario con comentarios sobre los libros.

Disfrute de la lectura. ¡Su niño, de seguro, también disfrutará!

Atentamente,

GRADE K: REPRODUCIBLE FICTION BOOKMARKS

Share these bookmarks with your children to remind them of some key features of different fiction genres.

Read Fiction

✓ Look at the cover.

✓ Say the name of the book.

✓ Look at the pictures.

✓ Read the story.

✓ See what happens first.

✓ See what happens last.

Read a Fairy Tale

✓ Say the name of the book.

✓ Flip through the book.

✓ Look for things that are not real.

✓ Read the story.

✓ Think about where the story takes place.

✓ Look for a happy ending.

Read a Poem

✓ Read the name of the poem.

✓ Read the poem aloud.

✓ Hear words that sound the same.

✓ Hear a pattern.

✓ Think about the words.

Read a Fantasy

✓ Look at the cover.

✓ Say the name of the book.

✓ Look at the pictures.

✓ Look for things that could not happen in real life.

MARCADORES DE GÉNERO REPRODUCIBLES

Reparta estos marcadores a sus alumnos para que recuerden algunas de las características más importantes de los géneros de ficción.

Al leer un cuento de ficción

✓ Mira la portada.

✓ Di el nombre del libro.

✓ Mira los dibujos.

✓ Lee el cuento.

✓ Mira qué ocurre primero.

✓ Mira qué ocurre al final.

Al leer un cuento de hadas

✓ Di el nombre del libro.

✓ Hojea el libro.

✓ Busca cosas que no sean reales.

✓ Lee el cuento.

✓ Piensa en dónde ocurre el cuento.

✓ Busca el final feliz.

Al leer un poema

✓ Lee el nombre del poema.

✓ Lee el poema en voz alta.

✓ Pon atención a las palabras que suenen parecido.

✓ Oye el patrón.

✓ Piensa en las palabras.

Al leer un cuento de fantasía

✓ Mira la portada.

✓ Di el nombre del libro.

✓ Mira los dibujos.

✓ Busca cosas que no podrían ocurrir en la vida real.

GRADE 1: REPRODUCIBLE FICTION BOOKMARKS

Share these bookmarks with your children to remind them of some key features of different fiction genres.

Reading Fiction

✓ Look at the cover.
✓ Read the title.
✓ Look at the pictures.
✓ See who is in the story. See what they do.
✓ Read the story.
✓ Think about what happens first, next, last.

Reading a Fairy Tale

✓ Read the title.
✓ Flip through the book.
✓ Look for places, people, and animals that are not real.
✓ Read the story.
✓ Think about where the story takes place.
✓ Think about when the story takes place.
✓ Look for a happy ending.

Reading a Poem

✓ Read the title. Find out what the poem is about.
✓ Read the poem aloud.
✓ Listen for words that rhyme.
✓ Listen for a pattern in the words.
✓ Think about the pictures that the words make in your mind.

Reading Fantasy

✓ Read the title.
✓ Flip through the book.
✓ Look for things that could not happen in real life.
✓ Look for places that could not be real.
✓ Look for animals that act like people and talk in the story.

MARCADORES DE GÉNERO REPRODUCIBLES

Reparta estos marcadores a sus alumnos para que recuerden algunas de las características más importantes de los géneros de ficción.

Al leer un cuento de ficción

✓ Mira la portada.

✓ Lee el título.

✓ Mira los dibujos.

✓ Mira quiénes participan en el cuento. Mira qué hacen.

✓ Lee el cuento.

✓ Piensa en qué pasa primero, al medio y al final.

Al leer un cuento de hadas

✓ Lee el título.

✓ Hojea el libro.

✓ Busca lugares, personas y animales que no sean reales.

✓ Lee el cuento.

✓ Piensa en dónde ocurre el cuento.

✓ Piensa en cuándo ocurre el cuento.

✓ Busca el final feliz.

Al leer un poema

✓ Lee el título. Descubre de qué trata el poema.

✓ Lee el poema en voz alta.

✓ Pon atención a las palabras que riman.

✓ Busca un patrón en las palabras.

✓ Piensa en las cosas que te imaginas al leer.

Al leer un cuento de fantasía

✓ Lee el título.

✓ Hojea el libro.

✓ Busca cosas que no podrían ocurrir en la vida real.

✓ Busca lugares que no podrían ser reales.

✓ Busca animales que actúen como personas y que hablen.

GRADE 2: REPRODUCIBLE FICTION BOOKMARKS

Share these bookmarks with your children to remind them of some of the key features of different fiction genres.

Quick Clues for Reading Fiction

✓ Look at the cover.

✓ Read the title.

✓ Look for people in the story who are like real people.

✓ Read where the story happens, such as a school or a home.

✓ Find out what people do to fix problems.

Quick Clues for Reading a Fairy Tale

✓ Read the title.

✓ Look at the pictures. Look for places, people, and animals that are not real.

✓ Read the story.

✓ Read to find out where the story takes place.

✓ Think about when the story happens.

✓ Look for a happy ending.

Quick Clues for Reading a Mystery

✓ Read the title to find out what the mystery is.

✓ Read the story. Find out the puzzle or crime. See who wants to solve it.

✓ Look for clues to solve the mystery.

✓ Think about what will happen next.

Quick Clues for Reading a Poem

✓ Read the title. Find out what the poem is about.

✓ Read the poem aloud.

✓ Listen for a pattern in the sentences.

✓ Listen for a pattern in the words.

✓ Think about the pictures the words make in your mind.

Quick Clues for Reading a Fable

✓ Read the title. Look for names of animals.

✓ Read the story. See how the animals or objects talk.

✓ Read the end. Find out what happens to one of the animals.

✓ Think about the lesson learned.

Quick Clues for Reading Fantasy

✓ Look for people, animals, and places that are not real.

✓ Find out if there are animals that talk or people who travel in time.

✓ Find out what the problem is.

✓ Read to see how the problem is solved.

MARCADORES DE GÉNERO REPRODUCIBLES

Reparta estos marcadores a sus alumnos para que recuerden algunas de las características más importantes de los géneros de ficción.

Breves consejos para leer textos de ficción

✓ Mira la portada.

✓ Lee el título.

✓ En el cuento, busca personas que sean como las personas de verdad.

✓ Lee dónde ocurre la historia, por ejemplo, en una escuela o una casa.

✓ Descubre qué hace la gente para resolver los problemas.

Breves consejos para leer un cuento de hadas

✓ Lee el título.

✓ Mira los dibujos. Busca lugares, personas y animales que no sean reales.

✓ Lee el cuento.

✓ Lee para saber dónde ocurre la historia.

✓ Piensa cuándo ocurre la historia.

✓ Busca el final feliz.

Breves consejos para leer un cuento de misterio

✓ Lee el título para saber de qué trata el misterio.

✓ Lee el cuento. Descubre el acertijo o el crimen. Descubre quién quiere resolverlo.

✓ Busca pistas para resolver el misterio.

✓ Piensa qué ocurrirá después.

Breves consejos para leer un poema

✓ Lee el título. Descubre de qué trata el poema.

✓ Lee el poema en voz alta.

✓ Busca un patrón en las oraciones.

✓ Busca un patrón en las palabras.

✓ Piensa en las cosas que te imaginas al leer.

Breves consejos para leer una fábula

✓ Lee el título. Busca nombres de animales.

✓ Lee la historia. Fíjate cómo hablan los animales o los objetos.

✓ Lee el final. Descubre qué le ocurre a uno de los animales.

✓ Piensa en la lección aprendida.

Breves consejos para leer un cuento de fantasía

✓ Busca personas, animales y lugares que no sean reales.

✓ Fíjate si hay animales que hablan o gente que viaja en el tiempo.

✓ Descubre cuál es el problema.

✓ Lee para saber cómo se resuelve el problema.

GRADE 3: REPRODUCIBLE FICTION BOOKMARKS

Share these bookmarks with your students to remind them of some key features of different fiction genres.

Quick Clues for Reading Realistic Fiction

✓ Look at the cover and the title.

✓ Read the story. See if the characters are like real people.

✓ Look for where and when the story happens. See if it's like a real place.

✓ Read where the story happens, such as a school or a home.

✓ Find out what people do to solve their problems.

Quick Clues for Reading a Folktale

✓ Read the title. Think what the story is about.

✓ Read the story. See which characters are good and which are bad.

✓ Find out what the characters' goals are.

✓ Look for things that happen three times.

✓ Find out if the good characters reach their goals in the end. See what happens to the bad characters.

Quick Clues for Reading a Mystery

✓ Read the title to learn what the mystery is.

✓ Read the story to find the puzzle or crime and who wants to solve it.

✓ Look for clues to solve the mystery.

✓ Think about events that are scary and can't be explained.

✓ Look for clues that help you guess what will happen next.

✓ See how the mystery is solved in the end.

Quick Clues for Reading a Poem

✓ Read the title. Think about what the topic of the poem is.

✓ Look at how many lines there are and if they are in groups.

✓ Read the poem aloud.

✓ Listen for a pattern in the words.

✓ Listen for a pattern in the sentences.

✓ Think about the pictures that form in your mind as you read.

Quick Clues for Reading a Play

✓ Read the title.

✓ Find a list of characters in the beginning.

✓ Read each act or part of the play. Note where each act takes place.

✓ Look for the names of characters and the words they say.

✓ Look for words that tell you how the characters speak and move.

Quick Clues for Reading Fantasy

✓ Read the title. Think what it tells you about the story.

✓ Read the story. Look for people, places, and animals that are not real.

✓ Look for animals that may talk and people who may travel in time.

✓ Find out what the problem is.

✓ Read to see how the problem is solved and if magic or magical thinking is used.

MARCADORES DE GÉNERO REPRODUCIBLES

Reparta estos marcadores a sus alumnos para que recuerden algunas de las características más importantes de los géneros de ficción.

Breves consejos para leer ficción realista

✓ Mira la portada y el título.

✓ Lee el cuento. Fíjate si los personajes son como las personas de verdad.

✓ Busca dónde y cuándo ocurre la historia. Piensa si es como un lugar real.

✓ Lee dónde ocurre la historia, por ejemplo, en una escuela o una casa.

✓ Averigua qué hace la gente para resolver los problemas.

Breves consejos para leer un cuento folclórico

✓ Lee el título. Piensa sobre qué trata el cuento.

✓ Lee el cuento. Piensa qué personajes son buenos y cuáles son malos.

✓ Descubre cuáles son las metas de los personajes.

✓ Busca cosas que ocurran tres veces.

✓ Descubre si al final los personajes buenos alcanzan sus metas. Lee qué les ocurre a los personajes malos.

Breves consejos para leer un cuento de misterio

✓ Lee el título para saber de qué trata el misterio.

✓ Lee el cuento para hallar el acertijo o problema y quiénes desean resolverlo.

✓ Busca pistas para resolver el misterio.

✓ Piensa en los eventos aterradores que no se puedan explicar.

✓ Busca pistas para adivinar qué va a ocurrir.

✓ Descubre cómo se resuelve el misterio al final del cuento.

Breves consejos para leer un poema

✓ Lee el título. Piensa cuál es el tema del poema.

✓ Mira cuántas líneas tiene el poema y si están en grupos.

✓ Lee el poema en voz alta.

✓ Busca un patrón en las palabras.

✓ Busca un patrón en las oraciones.

✓ Piensa qué te imaginas al leer el poema.

Breves consejos para leer una obra de teatro

✓ Lee el título.

✓ Busca la lista de personajes al principio de la obra.

✓ Lee todos los actos o partes de la obra. Fíjate dónde ocurre cada acto.

✓ Busca los nombres de los personajes y lo que dicen.

✓ Busca palabras que te indiquen cómo hablan y se mueven los personajes.

Breves consejos para leer un cuento de fantasía

✓ Lee el título. Piensa qué te indica sobre el cuento.

✓ Lee el cuento. Busca personas, lugares y animales que no sean reales.

✓ Busca animales que hablen o personas que viajen en el tiempo.

✓ Descubre cuál es el problema.

✓ Lee para saber cómo se resuelve el problema y si se usó magia para hacerlo.

GRADE 4: REPRODUCIBLE FICTION BOOKMARKS

Share these bookmarks with your students to remind them of some key features of different fiction genres.

Quick Clues for Reading Realistic Fiction

✓ Read the title. Think what the cover shows.

✓ Read the story. Meet the characters and learn about the setting.

✓ Note how characters are like real people with real problems.

✓ Follow the sequence of events. Predict what will happen next.

✓ Find out what people do to solve problems or reach goals.

Quick Clues for Reading a Novel

✓ Read the title and the author's name.

✓ Check how many chapters there are.

✓ Note the setting and the time covered by the story as you read.

✓ Note the main characters and what they are like.

✓ Follow the events, problems, and conflicts in the plot.

✓ Note how problems are solved in the end.

Quick Clues for Reading a Mystery

✓ Read the title to learn what the mystery is.

✓ Note the characters who want to solve the mystery and why.

✓ Look for clues to solve the mystery.

✓ Look for how the author builds suspense.

✓ Look for clues that help you guess what will happen next.

✓ See how the mystery is solved in the end.

Quick Clues for Reading Historical Fiction

✓ Read the title and the author's name.

✓ Note when and where in history the story takes place.

✓ Read the story. Imagine how people lived in this time.

✓ See how characters take part in historical events.

✓ Compare how people in the past solve problems with what people do today.

Quick Clues for Reading a Play

✓ Read the title and the playwright's name.

✓ Read the list of characters' names in the beginning.

✓ Note where each act of the play takes place.

✓ Look for characters' names before the words they say.

✓ Note words that explain how the characters speak and move.

Quick Clues for Reading a Fable

✓ Read the title and the author's name. Aesop is the author of many fables.

✓ Note if the characters are animals.

✓ See if one character tries to trick or outsmart another character.

✓ Decide what the problem is.

✓ See who learns a lesson in the end. Decide what the lesson is.

MARCADORES DE GÉNERO REPRODUCIBLES

Reparta estos marcadores a sus alumnos para que recuerden algunas de las características más importantes de los géneros de ficción.

Breves consejos para leer ficción realista

✓ Lee el título. Piensa qué muestra la portada.

✓ Lee el cuento. Conoce los personajes y el ambiente.

✓ Fíjate que los personajes son como las personas reales y que tienen problemas de verdad.

✓ Sigue la secuencia de sucesos. Predice qué ocurrirá después.

✓ Descubre qué hace la gente para resolver los problemas o alcanzar sus metas.

Breves consejos para leer una novela

✓ Lee el título y el nombre del autor.

✓ Explora cuántos capítulos hay.

✓ Al leer, pon atención al ambiente y a la época de la historia.

✓ Fíjate en los personajes principales y en lo que hacen.

✓ Pon atención a los sucesos, problemas y conflictos de la trama.

✓ Descubre cómo se resuelven los problemas al final.

Breves consejos para leer un cuento de misterio

✓ Lee el título para saber de qué trata el misterio.

✓ Fíjate en los personajes que quieren resolver el misterio y por qué quieren hacerlo.

✓ Busca pistas para resolver el misterio.

✓ Fíjate en cómo el autor crea suspenso.

✓ Busca pistas para adivinar qué ocurrirá después.

✓ Descubre cómo se resuelve el misterio al final.

Breves consejos para leer ficción histórica

✓ Lee el título y el nombre del autor.

✓ Fíjate en qué momento y lugar de la historia ocurre el cuento.

✓ Lee el cuento. Imagina cómo vivía la gente en esa época.

✓ Observa cómo los personajes participan en acontecimientos históricos.

✓ Compara cómo se resolvían los problemas en el pasado y cómo se resuelven hoy en día.

Breves consejos para leer una obra de teatro

✓ Lee el título y el nombre del dramaturgo.

✓ Lee la lista de personajes al principio de la obra.

✓ Fíjate dónde ocurre cada acto de la obra.

✓ Busca los nombres de los personajes antes de sus diálogos.

✓ Pon atención a las palabras que indican cómo hablan y se mueven los personajes.

Breves consejos para leer una fábula

✓ Lee el título y el nombre del autor. Esopo es autor de muchas fábulas.

✓ Fíjate si los personajes son animales.

✓ Piensa si un personaje trata de engañar o burlar a otro.

✓ Descubre cuál es el problema.

✓ Descubre quién aprende una lección al final de la fábula. Decide cuál fue esa lección.

GRADE 5: REPRODUCIBLE FICTION BOOKMARKS

Share these bookmarks with your students to remind them of some key features of different fiction genres.

Quick Clues for Reading Realistic Fiction

- ✓ Read the title and the author's name.
- ✓ Look for characters who are as believable as real people.
- ✓ Note if the problems characters have and the actions they take to solve them seem truthful.
- ✓ Decide if the outcomes are reasonable. Think about whether this could happen in real life.
- ✓ Think about the ending and decide if it is satisfactory.

Quick Clues for Reading a Novel

- ✓ Read the title and the author's name. Learn about the story on the back cover or book jacket.
- ✓ Note the setting and the time frame the story covers as you read.
- ✓ Look for major and minor characters and their role in the story.
- ✓ Follow the sequence of events and conflicts in the plot. Note if there are subplots.
- ✓ Decide if conflicts are resolved in the end.

Quick Clues for Reading a Mystery

- ✓ Read the title for a clue to what the mystery is.
- ✓ Note the characters who want to solve the mystery and why.
- ✓ Note how suspense builds as characters look for clues.
- ✓ Look for clues that foreshadow what will happen next.
- ✓ Find out in the end if the mystery is solved as you thought or if the ending is a surprise.

Quick Clues for Reading Historical Fiction

- ✓ Read the title and the author's name.
- ✓ Note when and where in history the story takes place.
- ✓ Note people's clothing, food, and homes. See what kind of work they do.
- ✓ See how characters take part in historical events.
- ✓ Look for how the setting affects what happens to the characters.

Quick Clues for Reading Science Fiction

- ✓ Read the title and the author's name.
- ✓ Find out if the story happens in the future and on another planet.
- ✓ Note details of the world in which the characters live.
- ✓ Look for scientific ideas that influence the plot.
- ✓ Read to see how characters solve problems and conflicts in this world.

Quick Clues for Reading a Legend

- ✓ Read the title to find what hero the story will be about.
- ✓ Read the story to discover what amazing deeds the hero did.
- ✓ Decide which deeds are more realistic and might be based on a real person in history.
- ✓ Note the conflicts and the problems.
- ✓ Think about what the hero's goal is and if this goal is reached.

MARCADORES DE GÉNERO REPRODUCIBLES

Reparta estos marcadores a sus alumnos para que recuerden algunas de las características más importantes de los géneros de ficción.

Breves consejos para leer ficción realista

✓ Lee el título y el nombre del autor.

✓ Busca personajes que parezcan personas reales.

✓ Determina si los problemas que tienen los personajes y las decisiones que toman para resolverlos parecen verídicos.

✓ Decide si los resultados son razonables. Piensa si esto podría ocurrir en la vida real.

✓ Piensa en el final y determina si es satisfactorio.

Breves consejos para leer una novela

✓ Lee el título y el nombre del autor. Lee la contraportada o sobrecubierta para aprender más del libro.

✓ Mientras lees, fíjate en el ambiente y periodo de tiempo en que ocurre la historia.

✓ Busca los personajes principales y secundarios y su papel en la historia.

✓ Sigue la secuencia de sucesos y los conflictos de la trama. Fíjate si hay historias secundarias.

✓ Decide si al final los conflictos se resuelven o no.

Breves consejos para leer un cuento de misterio

✓ Lee el título para saber de qué trata el misterio.

✓ Fíjate en los personajes que quieren resolver el misterio y por qué quieren hacerlo.

✓ Nota que hay más misterio a medida que los personajes buscan pistas.

✓ Busca pistas que predigan qué sucederá después.

✓ Al final, descubre si el misterio se resolvió como pensabas o si fue una sorpresa.

Breves consejos para leer ficción histórica

✓ Lee el título y el nombre del autor.

✓ Fíjate cuándo y dónde ocurre la historia.

✓ Presta atención a la vestimenta, alimentos y viviendas de la gente. Fíjate en qué trabajan.

✓ Lee cómo los personajes participan en acontecimientos históricos.

✓ Presta atención a cómo el ambiente afecta lo que les ocurre a los personajes.

Breves consejos para leer ciencia ficción

✓ Lee el título y el nombre del autor.

✓ Averigua si la historia ocurre en el futuro o en otro planeta.

✓ Fíjate en los detalles del mundo en que viven los personajes.

✓ Busca ideas científicas que influyan en la trama.

✓ Al leer, descubre cómo los personajes resuelven problemas y conflictos en ese mundo.

Breves consejos para leer una leyenda

✓ Lee el título para descubrir sobre qué héroe tratará la historia.

✓ Lee la historia para descubrir qué hazañas realizó ese héroe.

✓ Decide cuáles hazañas son más realistas y podrían basarse en una persona verdadera.

✓ Pon atención a los conflictos y a los problemas.

✓ Piensa cuál es la meta del héroe y si la alcanza.

GRADE 6: REPRODUCIBLE FICTION BOOKMARKS

Share these bookmarks with your students to remind them of some key features of different fiction genres.

Quick Clues for Reading a Graphic Novel

- ✓ Read the title and the author's name.
- ✓ Preview the pictures, or graphic part of the novel, before you start reading.
- ✓ Find characters' words in the speech balloons.
- ✓ Look for how characters feel in the illustrations.
- ✓ Find descriptions of what happens in the text boxes on the illustrations.
- ✓ Follow the story sequence by moving from panel to panel.

Quick Clues for Reading a Novel

- ✓ Read the title and the author's name. Learn about the story on the back cover or book jacket.
- ✓ Decide where and when the story takes place as you begin to read.
- ✓ Identify the major and minor characters and the problems or conflicts they have.
- ✓ Follow the rising action in the plot.
- ✓ Decide where the story climax is and what resolution follows at the end.

Quick Clues for Reading a Poem

- ✓ Read the title to learn what the poem is about.
- ✓ Listen for rhyme and/or rhythm as you read.
- ✓ Determine the emotion the poet expresses.
- ✓ Decide what kind of poem it is, depending on length, the rhythm, number of lines, and syllables per line.
- ✓ Pay attention to the images the words create in your mind.

Quick Clues for Reading Historical Fiction

- ✓ Read the title and the author's name.
- ✓ Note the historical setting for the story.
- ✓ Pay attention to details of clothing, food preparation, and transportation to get a sense of the time period.
- ✓ Note any names of real places and real people in history.
- ✓ Decide how the setting influences the plot and the characters' actions.

Quick Clues for Reading Science Fiction

- ✓ Read the title for clues to what the story is about.
- ✓ Decide what the setting is: another planet, a spaceship, and/or the future.
- ✓ Note how the setting is different from the world in which you live.
- ✓ Decide how science or futuristic technology influences the plot.
- ✓ Follow the plot to identify conflicts and how they are resolved in the end.

Quick Clues for Reading a Myth

- ✓ Read the title to learn who and what the story is about.
- ✓ Read the story to decide what natural event or human question might be explained.
- ✓ Identify the setting and the culture the myth comes from.
- ✓ Look for human characters who may interact with gods and goddesses or mythical creatures.
- ✓ Note how conflicts are resolved.

MARCADORES DE GÉNERO REPRODUCIBLES

Reparta estos marcadores a sus alumnos para que recuerden algunas de las características más importantes de los géneros de ficción.

Breves consejos para leer una novela gráfica

✓ Lee el título y el nombre del autor.

✓ Antes de comenzar a leer, revisa las ilustraciones, o parte gráfica de la novela.

✓ Lee lo que dicen los personajes en los globos de diálogo.

✓ Mira las ilustraciones para saber cómo se sienten los personajes.

✓ Lee las descripciones de lo que pasa en las cajas de texto.

✓ Para seguir la secuencia de la historia lee de panel a panel.

Breves consejos para leer una novela

✓ Lee el título y el nombre del autor. Lee la contraportada o sobrecubierta para aprender más sobre el libro.

✓ Mientras lees, fíjate dónde y cuándo ocurre la historia.

✓ Identifica los personajes principales y secundarios y sus problemas o conflictos.

✓ Sigue el desarrollo de la acción en la trama.

✓ Decide cuál es el climax de la historia y cuál es la resolución final.

Breves consejos para leer un poema

✓ Lee el título para saber de qué trata el poema.

✓ Mientras lees, presta atención a la rima o al ritmo.

✓ Determina qué emoción expresa el poeta.

✓ Identifica qué tipo de poema es, de acuerdo al largo, rit,mo, número de versos y sílabas por verso.

✓ Presta atención a las imágenes que las palabras crean en tu mente.

Breves consejos para leer ficción histórica

✓ Lee el título y el nombre del autor.

✓ Fíjate en el ambiente histórico del cuento.

✓ Para entender la época, fíjate en detalles como la vestimenta, la preparación de los alimentos y los medios de transporte.

✓ Fíjate en los nombres de lugares y personas verdaderos en la historia.

✓ Decide cómo el ambiente influye en la trama y en las acciones de los personajes.

Breves consejos para leer ciencia ficción

✓ Lee el título para comprender sobre qué trata la historia.

✓ Identifica el ambiente: otro planeta, una nave espacial y/o el futuro.

✓ Fíjate cómo el ambiente es distinto del mundo en que vives.

✓ Decide cómo la ciencia o la tecnología futurista influye en la trama.

✓ Sigue la trama para identificar conflictos y cómo éstos se resuelven al final.

Breves consejos para leer mitos

✓ Lee el título para que sepas sobre quién o qué trata la historia.

✓ Lee la historia para identificar qué evento natural o pregunta se explica.

✓ Identifica el ambiente y la cultura de la cual proviene el mito.

✓ Fíjate en personajes humanos que interactúen con dioses o personajes míticos.

✓ Presta atención a cómo se resuelven los conflictos.

REPRODUCIBLE NONFICTION BOOKMARKS

Share these bookmarks with your students to remind them of some of the key features of nonfiction text.

Quick Clues for Reading Nonfiction

✓ Preview the piece.

✓ Read the title, introduction, and headings to discover the main ideas.

✓ Make a prediction about the subject of the piece.

✓ Pay special attention to bold-faced words and extra graphic features.

✓ Study the graphic aids and read the captions carefully.

Quick Clues for Reading Maps

✓ Read the map title.

✓ Find the symbols.

✓ Look at the map key. Read the labels.

✓ Find the map scale.

✓ Find the compass rose.

Quick Clues for Reading Primary Sources

✓ First, read the title.

✓ Preview the text to learn about the topic.

✓ Read the main article.

✓ Read the primary source material. Ask yourself, "How does this information add to what I know about the topic?"

Quick Clues for Reading Graphs

✓ Read the title of the graph.

✓ Think about the topic.

✓ Look at each part of the graph and read each label.

✓ Think about what information is being represented.

✓ Look at the labels. Think about what the numbers stand for.

✓ For line graphs, use your finger to trace from each dot to the side and the bottom.

Quick Clues for Reading Reference Sources

✓ Look up your topic in the table of contents or index.

✓ Preview the text.

✓ Use the special features as you read.

✓ Think about how the information from the source fits with what you know.

Quick Clues for Reading Magazine Articles

✓ Read the title, deck, and subheadings to learn the main ideas.

✓ Predict what the article will be about.

✓ Notice any special features.

✓ Pay attention to bold-faced words.

✓ Study the graphic aids and read the captions carefully.

MARCADORES DE LIBROS REPRODUCIBLES

Reparta estos marcadores entre sus alumnos para que recuerden algunas de las características más importantes de los textos de no ficción.

Breves consejos para leer textos de no ficción

✓ Hojea el artículo.

✓ Lee el título, la introducción y los encabezamientos para determinar la idea principal.

✓ Haz una predicción sobre el tema del artículo.

✓ Presta especial atención a las palabras en negrita u otras características sobresalientes.

✓ Observa las gráficas y lee los pies de grabado detenidamente.

Breves consejos para leer mapas

✓ Lee el título del mapa.

✓ Busca los símbolos del mapa.

✓ Observa la leyenda del mapa.

✓ Lee los rótulos.

✓ Busca la escala.

✓ Busca la rosa náutica.

Breves consejos para leer fuentes de información

✓ Primero, lee el título.

✓ Haz una lectura preliminar del texto para tener una idea del tema.

✓ Lee el artículo principal.

✓ Mientras lees, pregúntate qué nueva información has aprendido sobre el tema.

Breves consejos para leer gráficas

✓ Lee el título de la gráfica. Piensa sobre el tema.

✓ Observa cada sección de la gráfica y lee cada rótulo.

✓ Piensa en la información que se presenta en la gráfica.

✓ Observa los rótulos. Piensa en qué significan los números que aparecen.

✓ En las gráficas lineales, marca con el dedo las líneas que van de cada punto a las coordenadas.

Breves consejos para leer fuentes de referencia

✓ Busca el tema de interés en la tabla de contenido o en el índice.

✓ Haz una lectura preliminar del texto.

✓ A medida que leas, ten en cuenta características especiales.

✓ Analiza si la información que aparece en esta fuente es la que necesitas.

Breves consejos para leer artículos de revista

✓ Lee el título, la introducción y los subtítulos para determinar la idea principal.

✓ Haz una predicción sobre el tema del artículo.

✓ Observa cualquier característica especial.

✓ Presta atención a las palabras en negrita.

✓ Estudia las gráficas y lee los rótulos detenidamente.

Skills & Strategies Chart

Level	Title	Series	Author	Genre	Comprehension Strategies	Phonics and Word Study	Writing Options	Technology
A	Boxes		Avelyn Davidson	Realistic Fiction	Using Illustrations	Telling Sentences	descriptive label	www.artistshelpingchildren.org/boxesartscraftsideaskidsboxprojects.html
A	Helping		Linda Johns	Realistic Fiction	Developing Print Awareness	Initial Sounds	descriptive journal	http://www.atozteacherstuff.com/Tips/Classroom_Jobs/
A	Hop, Skip, and Jump		Janelle Cherrington	Realistic Fiction	Developing Print Awareness	Oral Blending of Sounds	descriptive narrative	http://www.gameskidsplay.net
A	Little Animals		Janet Reed	Fantasy	Understanding Genre: Fantasy	Beginning Consonants	expository descriptive	http://www.kidsrunning.com/
A	My Dog Fluffy		Janelle Cherrington	Informational Text	Using Punctuation	Naming Words	descriptive narrative	http://www.kindnews.org/teacher_zone/lesson_plans.asp
A	My House		Catherine Peters	Informational Text	Recognizing Sequence	Beginning Sounds	descriptive graphic aid	http://www.contractor.edu/buildhouselp/welcome.html
A	Playing		Avelyn Davidson	Realistic Fiction	Recognizing Patterned Text	Pictures and Word Structure	expository narrative	http://www.gameskidsplay.net/
A	Run, Rabbit!		Yael Landman	Realistic Fiction	Using Punctuation	High-Frequency Words	narrative expository	http://www.hsus.org/wildlife/a_closer_look_at_wildlife/rabbits.html
A	Storm, The		Avelyn Davidson	Informational Text	Activating Prior Knowledge	High-Frequency Words	list graphic aid	http://www.nws.noaa.gov/om/reachout/thunder-storm.shtml
A	Time		Avelyn Davidson	Realistic Fiction	Understanding Sequence	Phonogram -ug	descriptive narrative	http://www.time-for-time.com/lesson1.htm
B	Ants Go Home, The		Linda Johns	Fantasy	Understanding Sequence	High-Frequency Words	descriptive expository	http://www.pestworldforkids.org/ants.html
B	Fishing		Janet Reed	Fantasy	Recognizing Story Pattern	Beginning and Ending Sounds	list narrative	http://www.mbayaq.org/lc/kids_place/
B	Getting There		Edwin Johns	Nonfiction	Understanding Photographs	Initial Consonant Sounds	expository descriptive	www.atozkidstuff.com/tran.html
B	Home Run!		Catherine Peters	Realistic Fiction	Recognizing Setting	Words With Phonogram -it	narrative expository	http://www.theteacherscorner.net/printable-worksheets/seasonal/baseball/index.htm
B	Let's Play		Catherine Peters	Realistic Fiction	Reading Sentences	Words With Consonants	narrative list	www.education.com/reference/article/Ref_Developing_Language/
B	Look at Us		Linda Johns	Realistic Fiction	Identifying Setting	Sentence Structure	descriptive expository	http://www.edheads.org/activities/simple%2Dmachines/
B	My Feet		Janet Reed	Realistic Fiction	Making Predictions	High-Frequency Words	expository list	teachers-subject-guides.suite101.com/article.cfm/kindergarten_physical_education
B	Night Shift	Brain Bank	Ryan Josh	Nonfiction	Recognizing Patterned Text	Naming Words	expository graphic aid	www.teacher.scholastic.com/commclub/index.htm
B	Off to the City		Avelyn Davidson	Fantasy	Identifying Sequence	Words With Short a	narrative poster	www.bicyclinginfo.org/education/children-5to8.cfm
B	Zebras Don't Brush Their Teeth!	Brain Bank	Lynette Evans	Nonfiction	Comparing and Contrasting	Action Words	expository list	www.redcross.org/services/hss/resources/scrubby_bear_personal_hygiene.pdf
C	Big Blue Sea, The	Brain Bank	Janine Scott	Informational Text	Recognizing Patterned Text	Compound Words	descriptive expository	http://www.ceismc-gatech.edu/busyt/bio_marine.shtml
C	Brave Dave and the Dragons		Janet Reed	Fantasy	Making Predictions	Words With Consonants	expository narrative	www.educatall.com/page/19/Knights-and-prin-cesses.html

Level	Title	Series	Author	Genre	Comprehension Strategies	Phonics and Word Study	Writing Options	Technology
C	Hide and Seek		Janet Reed	Fantasy	Recognizing Questions	Describing Words	graphic aid / descriptive	www.gameskidsplay.net
C	It's Time to Eat!		Avelyn Davidson	Informational Text	Reading Questions and Answers	Punctuation	expository / descriptive	http://www.sandiegozoo.org/animalbytes/index.html
C	Little Blue Fish		Lynette Evans	Realistic Fiction	Recognizing Setting	Punctuation	narrative / expository	http://www.fi.edu/fellows/fellow8/dec98/intera.html
C	Little Duckling Is Lost		May Nelson	Fantasy	Recognizing Patterned Text	Initial Consonants	descriptive / narrative	http://www.eastvalleywildlife.org/ducks.htm
C	Oak Street Party, The		Catherine Peters	Realistic Fiction	Comparing and Contrasting	Apostrophe *s*	descriptive / list	http://www.crayola.com/lesson-plans/detail/community-celebrations-3-d-timeline-lesson-plan/
C	One Frog, One Fly		Wendy Blaxland	Fantasy	Understanding Genre: Fantasy	Describing Words	narrative / expository	http://www.picadome.fcps.net/lab/curr1/food_chain/default.htm
C	Pass the Pasta, Please!		Linda Johns	Informational Text	Recognizing Punctuation	Initial Consonant Sounds	descriptive / graphic aid	http://www.ilovepasta.org/shapes.html
C	Patterns	Emergent Reader	Samantha Berger, Daniel Moreton	Informational Text	Using Picture Details	Plurals	descriptive / list	http://www.uen.org/themepark/patterns/nature-patterns.shtml
D	After School Fun		May Nelson	Realistic Fiction	Identifying Setting	Initial Consonants	labeling / narrative	http://www.exploratorium.edu/afterschool/index.html
D	Dog Walker, The		Janet Reed	Realistic Fiction	Comparing and Contrasting	Exclamation Points	narrative / description	http://dogplay.com/youth.html
D	Little Red Hen, The		retold by Janelle Cherrington	Traditional Literature	Recognizing Patterned Text	Words With Short Vowels	labeling / descriptive	www.grainchain.com/5-to-7/Where-does-bread-come-from/Default.aspx
D	Little Turtle, The		Vachel Lindsay	Poem	Recognizing Sequence	Words With r-Controlled Vowels	descriptive / list	http://www.sandiegozoo.org/animalbytes/t-turtle.html
D	Noisy Breakfast, The		Ellen Blonder	Fantasy	Recognizing Story Pattern	Words With Short *i*	narrative / graphic aid	http://kidshealth.org/kid/stay_healthy/food/pyramid.html
D	Rainy Day, A		Lynette Evans	Realistic Fiction	Making Predictions	Compound Words	narrative / list	http://www.animalcorner.co.uk
D	Wake Up, Wake Up!		Brian & Rebecca Wildsmith	Humorous Fiction	Recognizing Sentence Pattern	Onomatopoeia	narrative / descriptive	http://www.kidsfarm.com/farm.htm
D	What Do You See? A Book About the Seasons		Sara Shapiro	Science Nonfiction	Summarizing	Words With Long *e*	labeling / descriptive	http://www.instructorweb.com/lesson/seasons.asp
D	Where in the World?	Brain Bank	May Nelson	Informational Text	Making Predictions	Short Vowels	descriptive / graphic aid	http://www.educationworld.com/a_lesson/archives/state.shtml
D	Who Lives Here?		Janet Reed	Realistic Fiction	Activating Prior Knowledge	Consonant Blends	descriptive / graphic aid	www.ecokidsonline.com/pub/eco_info/topics/canadas_north
E	Flap and Sing: Birds	Investigators	Ian Douglas	Narrative Nonfiction	Sequencing	Describing Words	descriptive / narrative	http://www.aviary.org/index.php
E	Fred's Wish for Fish		Yael Landman	Realistic Fiction	Reading Everyday Speech	Words With Digraphs	narrative / descriptive	http://pbskids.org/itsmylife/family/pets/article5.html
E	Fresh Fall Leaves		Betsy Franco	Realistic Fiction	Using Illustrations	Words With -ing	expository / descriptive	http://www.amug.org/~ibpratt/education/mypages/autumnleaves.html
E	I Go With Grandpa		Yael Landman	Realistic Fiction	Comparing and Contrasting	Short Vowel *u*	labeling / narrative	http://www.instructorweb.com/lesson/seasons.asp
E	Let's Play Soccer		Ian Douglas	Informational Text	Recognizing Patterned Text	Verbs	expository / descriptive	www.education.com/reference/article/Ref_Developing_Language/
E	Living Things	Brain Bank	Dorothy Avery	Science Nonfiction	Understanding Categorizing	Pronouns	expository / graphic aid	http://www.fi.edu/tfi/units/life/classify/classify.html
E	Magic Pot, The		Laura Smith	Fantasy	Understanding Genre: Fantasy	Words With /ou/	narrative / expository	www.goodcharacter.com/Estopics.html
E	No Snacks, Jack!		Janet Reed	Realistic Fiction	Understanding Cause and Effect	Contractions	narrative / persuasive	www.crayola.com/lesson-plans/detail/happy-healthy-habits-lesson-plan/

Level	Title	Series	Author	Genre	Comprehension Strategies	Phonics and Word Study	Writing Options	Technology
E	Painting		Janine Scott	Realistic Fiction	Analyzing Character	End Punctuation	expository descriptive	www.coe.ufl.edu/courses/eec6304/paint.htm
E	Yard Sale, The		Janelle Cherrington	Realistic Fiction	Making Predictions	Naming Words	labeling narrative	http://www.cambriarecycles.org/Reuse/YardSale.htm
F	Biscuit Visits the Big City		Alyssa Satin Capucilli	Realistic Fiction	Understanding Setting	Words That Describe	narrative expository	http://www.alyssacapucilli.com/
F	Bug, a Bear, and a Boy, A		David McPhail	Fantasy	Distinguishing Fantasy/Reality	Picture Details	narrative descriptive	http://www.edutopia.org/common-ground
F	Country Mouse and the Town Mouse, The		retold by Janet Reed	Traditional Literature/Fable	Understanding Genre: Fable	Reading Punctuation	persuasive narrative	www.learningtogive.org/lessons/unit83/lesson3.html
F	Go Home, Daisy		Barbara Hill	Realistic Fiction	Making Predictions	Action Words	expository descriptive	http://www.petclub.org/lost_pets.htm
F	Goldilocks and the Three Bears		retold by Sara Shapiro	Traditional Literature/Folktale	Reading Dialogue	Words With ou	expository letter	http://www.atozteacherstuff.com/pages/315.shtml
F	How Lizard Lost His Colors		retold by Sara Shapiro	Traditional Literature/Folktale	Understanding Cause and Effect	Words With ow	narrative expository	http://teacher.scholastic.com/writewit/mff/folk-talewshop_index.htm
F	Loose Tooth		Lola M. Schaefer	Realistic Fiction	Summarizing	Words With Vowels oo	narrative graphic aid	http://www.ada.org/public/education/teachers/ideas.asp
F	Meg and the Lost Pencil Case		Greg Parasmo	Realistic Fiction	Understanding Problems and Solutions	Suffix -ed	narrative expository	http://4h.missouri.edu/go/programs/character/resources/schoolstages.pdf
F	Melt It, Shape It: Glass	Investigators	May Nelson	Narrative Nonfiction	Reading for Information	Consonant Blends	expository descriptive	http://www.glassforever.co.uk/
F	Todd's Teacher		Janelle Cherrington	Realistic Fiction	Understanding Setting	Consonant Blends	narrative expository	www2.scholastic.com/browse/lessonplan.jsp?id=219
G	At the Apple Farm		Rachel Albanese and Laura Smith	Informational Text	Recognizing Story Sequence	Words With Short a	graphic aid narrative	www.usapple.org/consumers/kids
G	Deep Blue Sea, The		Audrey Wood	Realistic Fiction	Understanding Patterned Text	Words With Consonant + le	narrative descriptive	www.audreywood.com/mac_site/auds_jumpstation/aud_jumpstation.htm
G	Gingerbread Man, The		retold by Janelle Cherrington	Traditional Literature	Understanding Plot	Past-Tense Words	narrative expository	http://www.atozteacherstuff.com/Themes/Gingerbread/
G	I Just Forgot	Little Critter	Mercer Mayer	Fantasy	Using Illustrations	Reading Action Words With -ed	letter expository	www.littlecritter.com/
G	In Our Yard		Janet Reed	Realistic Fiction	Summarizing	Words With /ou/	poetry expository	http://www.insectidentification.org/
G	Is This a Moose?		Jenny Armstrong	Science Nonfiction	Comparing and Contrasting	Question Sentences	expository graphic aid	www.nhptv.org/NATUREWORKS/nw4.htm.
G	Justin's New Bike		Barbara Hill	Realistic Fiction	Drawing Conclusions	Action Words With -ing	list expository	http://kidshealth.org/kid/watch/out/bike_safety.html
G	Rabbit's Party		Eve Bunting	Fantasy	Making Inferences	Short Vowels	list narrative	http://teacherlink.ed.usu.edu/TLresources/units/Byrnes-celebrations/bday.html
G	Three Billy Goats Gruff, The		retold by Sara Shapiro	Traditional Literature/Fairy Tale	Recognizing Sequence	Contractions	narrative expository	http://edsitement.neh.gov/view_lesson_plan.asp?id=387#LESSON5
G	Very Silly School, A		Janelle Cherrington	Fantasy	Distinguishing Fantasy from Reality	Words With Short i	description expository	http://pbskids.org/arthur/parentsteachers/activities/acts/imaginary_pets.html?cat=art
H	Aunt Maud's Mittens		Yael Landman	Humorous Fiction	Recognizing Sequence of Events	Multisyllabic Words	narrative list	http://www.atozkidsstuff.com/article15.html
H	Father Who Walked on His Hands, The		based on a story by Margaret Mahy	Realistic Fiction	Using Illustrations	Plurals	expository descriptive	www.khake.org/page64.html
H	Good Morning, Monday		Sheila Keenan	Realistic Fiction	Understanding Setting	Compound Words	expository descriptive	www2.scholastic.com/browse/article.jsp?id=11619

Level	Title	Series	Author	Genre	Comprehension Strategies	Phonics and Word Study	Writing Options	Technology
H	Hop! Spring! Leap! Animals That Jump		Fiona Bayrock	Science Nonfiction	Monitoring Comprehension	Consonant Blends With s	descriptive narrative	www.teachersdomain.org/resource/tdc02.sci.life.colt.move/
H	Little Red Riding Hood		retold by Sara Shapiro	Fairy Tale	Making Inferences	Words With oo	narrative descriptive	http://www.usm.edu/english/fairytales/lrrh/lrrh-home.htm
H	Sammy the Seal		Syd Hoff	Fantasy	Using Punctuation	Dialogue	description narrative	http://www.lpzoo.org/animals/index.html/
H	Sione's Talo		Lino Nelisi	Traditional Literature/Folktale	Drawing Conclusions	Action Words in Past Tense	descriptive narrative	www.aucklandmuseum.com/site_resources/library/Education/Teachers_Guide/Teacher Resources_Library/Social_Science/SocSci10PacificPath1_1_.pdf
H	Trains		Rachel Albanese	Informational Text	Relating to Personal Experience	Consonant Blends	descriptive narrative	http://www.academickids.com/encyclopedia/index.php/Trains
H	Unusual Show, An		Ellen Blonder	Fantasy	Comparing and Contrasting	Opposites	list expository	www.plcmc.org/Services/Storytimes_to_go!/pdfs/Getting%20Dressed.pdf
H	Why Did the Chicken Cross the Road?		Janet Reed	Fantasy	Making Inferences	Reading Words With /ou/	descriptive persuasive	http://www.moneyinstructor.com
I	Animals at Night	Now I Know	Melvin Berger and Gilda Berger	Informational Text	Understanding Genre: Informational Text	Contractions	narrative expository	http://kindernature.storycounty.com/display.aspx?DocID=2005418944
I	Dolphins and Porpoises	Now I Know	Melvin and Gilda Berger	Informational Text	Using Picture Clues	Consonant Blends	descriptive narrative	www.savethewhales.org/dolphins.html/
I	Fat Cat, The: A Danish Folktale		translated by Jack Kent	Traditional Literature/Folktale	Recognizing Patterned Text	Multisyllabic Words	letter list	http://oaks.nvg.org/danish-folktales.html
I	Mama Zooms		Jane Cowen-Fletcher	Fantasy	Monitoring Comprehension	Compound Words	descriptive narrative	http://primaryschool.suite101.com/article.cfm/easy_ways_to_encourage_imagination
I	Nana's Place		Akimi Gibson	Realistic Fiction	Making Inferences	Dialogue	narrative descriptive	http://www.childrensgrief.net/info.htm
I	Shoo, Fly Guy!		Tedd Arnold	Humorous Fiction	Recognizing Story Sequence	Exclamatory Sentences	narrative expository	http://bugguide.net/node/view/7266
I	Two Crazy Pigs		Karen Berman Nagel	Fantasy	Understanding Compare and Contrast	Words With -ing	graphic aid descriptive	http://teacher.scholastic.com/writeit/humor/teacher/humorwriting.htm
I	Wax Man, The		retold by Olga Loya	Traditional Literature/Folktale	Understanding Cause and Effect	Action Words	narrative expository	http://www.americanfolklore.net/bedtimestories.html.
I	We're Going On a Nature Hunt		Steve Metzger	Realistic Fiction	Understanding Sequence	Long i: Consonant + Final e Pattern	descriptive narrative	http://kidsactivities.suite101.com/article.cfm/scavenger_hunting
I	Wheels on the Race Car, The		Alex Zane	Fantasy	Recognizing Setting	Sound Words	persuasive narrative	www.wheelsontheracecar.com/interview.htm
J	Antonio's Music		Joanna Emery	Biography	Visualizing	Irregular Past-Tense Verbs	expository graphic aid	www.classicalarchives.com/bios/vivaldi_bio.html
J	Big, Brown Pot, The		Margaret Mahy	Humorous Fiction	Identifying Cause and Effect	Past-Tense Verbs	narrative descriptive	www.pbs.org/parents/parenthelpers/cooking.html
J	Big Cats	Investigators	Lynette Evans	Narrative Nonfiction	Comparing and Contrasting	Comparatives -er, -est	narrative graphic aid	www.bigcats.com
J	Big Smelly Bear		Britta Teckentrup	Fantasy	Understanding Plot	Words With -ed	list persuasive	http://www.cyh.sa.gov.au/HealthTopics/HealthTopicDetailsKids.aspx?p=335np=289d=2146
J	In the Barrio		Alma Flor Ada	Realistic Fiction	Categorizing Information	Unfamiliar Words	expository descriptive	http://www.sedl.org/scimath/pasopartners/senses/
J	Just Us Women		Jeannette Caines	Realistic Fiction	Making Inferences	Contractions	list narrative	http://www.kent.k12.wa.us/curriculum/tech/K6/5/Roadtrip/unit_planRoadTrip.doc
J	Kenny and the Little Kickers		Claudio Marzollo	Fantasy	Understanding Character	Dialogue	narrative persuasive	http://kidshealth.org/parent/emotions/feelings/self_esteem.html
J	Poppleton Has Fun	Poppleton	Cynthia Rylant	Fantasy	Using Illustrations	Compound Words	letter description	http://atozteacherstuff.com/Themes/Friendship/

Level	Title	Series	Author	Genre	Comprehension Strategies	Phonics and Word Study	Writing Options	Technology
J	Safety in Numbers	Investigators	Lynette Evans	Narrative Nonfiction	Generating Questions	Multiple-Meaning Words	expository narrative	www.sandiegozoo.org/animalbytes/got_questions_groups_list.html
J	Young Cam Jansen and the Spotted Cat Mystery	Young Cam Jansen	David A. Adler	Mystery	Understanding Chapters	Compound Words	narrative list	www.educationworld.com/a_tsl/archives/02-1/lesson036.shtm
K	Allie's Basketball Dream		Barbara E. Barber	Realistic Fiction	Understanding Visualizing	Compound Words	narrative persuasive	http://webtech.kennesaw.edu/reading/alliesdream.htm
K	Andy Shane and the Very Bossy Dolores Starbuckle		Jennifer Richard Jacobson	Realistic Fiction	Recognizing Story Structure	Diphthong ou	narrative list	http://www.bam.gov/sub_yourlife/yourlife_conflict.html
K	Don't Let the Pigeon Stay Up Late!		Mo Willems	Fantasy	Drawing Conclusions	Words With r-Controlled Vowels	narrative expository	www.childrenslit.com/childrenslit/mai_willems_mo.html
K	Frog Prince, The	Hello Reader	Edith H. Tarcov	Traditional Literature/ Fairy Tale	Recognizing Sequence	Consonant Blends	descriptive narrative	http://www.suelebeau.com/fairytales.htm
K	Great Gracie Chase, The: Stop that Dog!		Cynthia Rylant	Realistic Fiction	Understanding Cause and Effect	Past Tense With -ed	narrative expository	www.loveyourdog.com
K	Gym Teacher From the Black Lagoon, The	Black Lagoon	Mike Thaler	Fantasy	Recognizing Point of View	Contractions	narrative expository	www.yale.edu/ynhti/curriculum/units/2002/4/02.04.05.x.html
K	Ibis: A True Whale Story		John Himmelman	Fantasy	Identifying Author's Purpose	Multiple-Meaning Words	expository descriptive	www.nightheron.com/trees_activityguideibisthewhale.html
K	Johnny Appleseed		Eva Moore	Traditional Literature/Folktale	Understanding Cause and Effect	r-Controlled Vowels	expository poetry	http://www.appleseed.net
K	On My Way to Buy Eggs		Chih-Yuan Chen	Realistic Fiction	Understanding Figurative Language	Vowel Digraphs	descriptive narrative	http://www.brucevanpatter.com/funstuff.html
K	Three Days on a River in a Red Canoe		Vera B. Williams	Realistic Fiction	Recognizing Point of View	Compound Words	descriptive narrative	http://boatsafe.com/kids/knots.htm
L	Alligator Baby		Robert Munsch	Fantasy	Recognizing Story Pattern	Reading Words With -ed	narrative graphic aid	www.robertmunsch.com
L	Amelia Bedelia Under Construction	Amelia Bedelia	Herman Parish	Realistic Fiction	Understanding Illustrations	Homophones	expository narrative	www.educationworld.com/a_lesson/dailylp/dailylp/dailylp048.shtml
L	Anansi the Spider: A Tale from the Ashanti		Gerald McDermott	Traditional Literature	Using Illustrations	Words With Long o	list narrative	http://www2.scholastic.com/browse/search?query=folktales
L	Cam Jansen and the Secret Service Mystery	Cam Jansen	David Adler	Realistic Fiction/Mystery	Understanding Plot	Action Verbs	expository list	http://kids.mysterynet.com
L	Miss Nelson Has a Field Day		Harry Allard	Realistic Fiction	Making Predictions	Contractions	descriptive expository	www.ducksters.com/sports/footballrules.php
L	Picking Apples & Pumpkins		Amy & Richard Hutchings	Informational Text	Understanding Compare and Contrast	Compound Words	expository narrative	http://localfoods.about.com/od/searchbyregion/Search_Seasonal_Fruits_Vegetables_By_Region.htm
L	Ricky Ricotta's Mighty Robot vs. the Mecha-Monkeys from Mars		Dav Pilkey	Science Fiction	Drawing Conclusions	Contractions	narrative descriptive	http://spaceplace.nasa.gov/en/kids/
L	Triple Rotten Day, The	It's Robert (#16)	Barbara Seuling	Realistic Fiction	Making Predictions	Multisyllabic Words	narrative persuasive	http://www2.scholastic.com/browse/contributor.jsp?id=2379
L	Worst Day of My Life, The	Little Bill	Bill Cosby	Realistic Fiction	Understanding Plot as Problem and Solution	Compound Words	narrative list	www.educationworld.com/a_curr/strategy/strategy019.shtml
L	Young Thurgood Marshall: Fighter for Equality	Alexander	Eric Carpenter	Biography	Practice Summarizing	Proper Nouns	graphic aid expository	http://brownboard.org/
M	Alexander, Who's Not (Do you hear me? I mean it!) Going to Move	Alexander	Judith Viorst	Realistic Fiction	Understand Making Inferences	Possessive Words With 's	narrative expository	www.kidslife.com.au/article.asp?ContentID=helping_kids_cope_with_change
M	Case of the Food Fight, The	Jigsaw Jones Mystery (#28)	James Preller	Mystery	Understanding Cause and Effect	Onomatopoeia	descriptive expository	http://www.mysterynet.com/learn/

Level	Title	Series	Author	Genre	Comprehension Strategies	Phonics and Word Study	Writing Options	Technology
M	Dancing With the Indians		Angela Shelf Medearis	Poem	Making Inferences	Inflectional Ending -ing	poetry; descriptive	http://www.awesomelibrary.org/Classroom/Social_Studies/Multicultural/Native_American.html
M	How a House is Built		Gail Gibbons	Informational Text	Understanding Sequence	Context Clues	list; descriptive	www.historyforkids.org/learn/architecture/houses.htm
M	Ivy and Bean and the Ghost That Had to Go	Ivy + Bean (#2)	Annie Barrows	Humorous Fiction	Understanding Text Features	Consonant Blends: s + qu	descriptive; narrative	www.anniebarrows.com/ivyandbean/
M	New Coat for Anna, A		Harriet Ziefert	Historical Fiction	Understanding Historical Context	Context Clues	expository; descriptive	http://www.usmint.gov/kids/timeMachine/
M	Penguin and the Pea, The		Janet Perlman	Fractured Fairy Tale	Understanding Cause and Effect	Words With Suffix -ly	descriptive; narrative	www.britishcouncil.org/learnenglish-central-poems-fairy-tales.htm
M	Stink: The Incredible Shrinking Kid		Megan McDonald	Humorous Fiction	Understanding Puns	Words With Suffixes	graphic-narrative; descriptive	http://www.childdevelopmentinfo.com/parenting/self_esteem.shtml
M	Stuart Goes to School		Sara Pennypacker	Fantasy	Visualizing	Compound Words	expository; narrative	http://kidshealth.org/kid/feeling/home_family/moving.html
M	Vampires Don't Wear Polka Dots	Bailey School Kids (#1)	Debbie Dadey and Marcia Thornton Jones	Fantasy	Making Predictions	Compound Words	narrative; expository	http://www.nea.org/classmanagement/disck021113.html
N	Alfie the Apostrophe		Moira Rose Donahue	Fantasy	Understanding Main Idea and Details	Words With Apostrophes	descriptive; narrative	http://www.teachingideas.co.uk/english/contents09writingpunctuationgrammar.htm
N	Fables		Arnold Lobel	Traditional Literature/Fable	Understanding Genre	Words With -ed	graphic aid; persuasive	http://teacher.scholastic.com/writewit/mff/
N	Franny K. Stein, Mad Scientist: Frantastic Voyage	Franny K. Stein (#5)	Jim Benton	Science Fiction	Understanding Plot	Reading Difficult Words	expository; persuasive	http://inventions.about.com/od/kidinventions/ss/kid_inventors_U.htm
N	Lion Dancer: Ernie Wan's Chinese New Year		Kate Waters and Madeline Slovenz-Low	Nonfiction	Generating Questions	Multisyllabic Words	graphic aid; descriptive	http://crafts.kaboose.com/holidays/chinese_new_year.html
N	Mice and Beans		Pam Muñoz Ryan	Fantasy	Distinguishing Fantasy from Reality	Using a Pronunciation Guide	narrative; descriptive	http://www.readwritethink.org/lessons/lesson_view.asp?id=890
N	Our Crazy Class Election	Comic Guy	Tim Roland	Realistic Fiction	Understanding Figurative Language	Idioms	descriptive; persuasive	http://www.kidsvotingusa.org/
N	Spy in the White House, A	Capital Mysteries (#4)	Ron Roy	Mystery	Understanding Idioms	Multiple-Meaning Words	expository; narrative	http://www.yale.edu/ynhti/curriculum/units/1989/4/89.04.06.x.html
N	Suitcase		Mildred Pitts Walter	Realistic Fiction	Understanding Problems and Solutions	Words With the Letter x	narrative; list	ssw.unc.edu/jif/makingchoices/lesson-g4.htm
N	Wonderful Alexander and the Catwings	Catwings	Ursula K. LeGuin	Fantasy	Understanding Theme	Words With -y, -ly	narrative; expository	http://www.ursulakleguin.com
N	Zen Shorts		Jon J. Muth	Traditional Literature/Fable	Understanding Genre: Fable	Words With Prefixes un-, im-	expository; narrative	www.tricycle.com/special-section/bringing-up-buddhists-a-resource-guide
O	Amber Brown Is Green with Envy	Amber Brown	Paula Danziger	Realistic Fiction	Understanding Character	Reading Homophones	narrative; descriptive	http://www.edupaperback.org/showauth2.cfm?authid=25
O	Angel Child, Dragon Child		Michele Maria Surat	Realistic Fiction	Understanding Plot	Difficult Words	descriptive; expository	http://www.educationworld.com/a_lesson/lesson340.shtml
O	Can You Fly High, Wright Brothers?	Science SuperGiants	Melvin Berger and Gilda Berger	Biography	Understanding Sequence	Words With Suffixes	descriptive; expository	http://www.wright-brothers.org
O	Chocolate Fever		Robert Kimmel Smith	Fiction	Identifying Problem/Solution	Suffixes -less, -ness	expository; graphic aid	www.candyusa.org/Chocolate/default.asp
O	Jake Drake, Know-It-All		Andrew Clements	Realistic Fiction	Understanding Story Structure	Reading Words With -ing	list; descriptive	http://www.kidscorner.org/html/sciencefair.php
O	Lost Treasure of the Emerald Eye	Geronimo Stilton (#1)	Geronimo Stilton	Fantasy	Understanding Chapters	Words With Multiple Meanings	narrative; letter	http://www.scholastic.com/titles/geronimostilton
O	Patchwork Quilt, The		Valerie Flournoy	Realistic Fiction	Understanding Character	Diphthongs ou, ow	expository; descriptive	http://www.madison.k12.wi.us/tnl/detectives/kids/KIDS-000328.html

Level	Title	Series	Author	Genre	Comprehension Strategies	Phonics and Word Study	Writing Options	Technology
O	Pinduli		Janell Cannon	Trickster Tale	Understanding Cause and Effect	Suffixes -y and -ly	descriptive narrative	www.wku.edu/~mary.meredith/student.htm
O	Shark Lady: True Adventures of Eugenie Clark		Ann McGovern	Biography	Understanding Cause and Effect	Reading Compound Words	descriptive expository	www.marinebio.com/MarineBio/MindGames
O	Talented Clementine, The		Sara Pennypacker	Realistic Fiction	Making Predictions	Words With Soft c and Hard c	expository list	www.scholastic.com/titles/abbyhayes/brainwaves/talent.htm
P	Nina, the Pinta, and the Vanishing Treasure, The (Alec Flint Super Sleuth)	Alec Flint Mystery (#1)	Jill Santopolo	Mystery	Understanding Problems and Solutions	Synonyms	narrative expository	http://americanhistory.si.edu/kids/index.cfm
P	Countdown to the Year 1000	Dragon Slayers' Academy (#8)	Kate H. McMullan	Fantasy	Understanding Setting	Unusual Language	expository persuasive	http://www.historyforkids.org/learn/medieval/history/history.htm
P	Da Wild, Da Crazy, Da Vinci (Time Warp Trio)	Time Warp Trio	Jon Scieszka	Science Fiction	Understanding Visualizing	Suffixes	narrative expository	http://www.mos.org/leonardo
P	Helen Keller's Teacher		Margaret Davidson	Biography	Recognizing Setting	Context Clues	list expository	http://www.actionfund.org/ohsay/saysee18.htm
P	Koya DeLaney and the Good Girl Blues		Eloise Greenfield	Realistic Fiction	Understanding Author's Purpose	Challenging Words	narrative persuasive	http://kidshealth.org/parent/emotions/behavior/sportsmanship.html
P	Magic School Bus and the Science Fair Expedition, The	Magic School Bus	Joanna Cole	Science Nonfiction	Generating Questions	Multisyllabic Words	graphic aid expository	http://www.sciencebuddies.org/
P	Mariposa, La		Francisco Jiménez	Realistic Fiction	Making Inferences	Prefixes	narrative expository	http://teacher.scholastic.com/lessonrepro/lessonplans/instructor/science2.htm
P	Talking Eggs, The		Robert D. San Souci	Traditional Literature/Folktale	Understanding Genre: Folktale	Vowel Digraphs	expository narrative	http://www.content.scholastic.com/browse/unitplan
P	Who Stole The Wizard of Oz?		Avi	Mystery	Understanding Point of View	Multisyllabic Words	descriptive narrative	http://www.teachersfirst.com/100books.cfm
P	You Can't See Your Bones with Binoculars		Harriet Ziefert	Informational Text	Using Diagrams	Context Clues	expository narrative	www.newtonsapple.tv/TeacherGuide.php?id=1534
Q	Abby Takes a Stand		Patricia McKissack	Historical Fiction	Understanding Sequence	Context Clues	descriptive expository	www.sitins.com/timeline.shtml
Q	Amulet: Book One, The Stonekeeper	Amulet	Kazu Kibuishi	Fantasy/Graphic Novel	Making Predictions	Onomatopoeia	descriptive narrative	http://www.scholastic.com/graphix/
Q	Bunnicula: A Rabbit-Tale of Mystery	Bunnicula	James and Deborah Howe	Fantasy	Identifying Problem/Solution	Understanding Homophones	expository persuasive	http://www.bcplonline.org/kidspage/kids_howe.html
Q	Champ		Marcia Thornton Jones	Realistic Fiction	Understanding Problems and Solutions	Suffixes	narrative expository	http://www.MarciaTJones.com
Q	Just Juice		Karen Hesse	Realistic Fiction	Understanding Theme	Words With Multiple Meanings	expository narrative	http://www.pbs.org/wgbh/misunderstoodminds/
Q	Life and Times of the Peanut, The		Charles Micucci	Informational Text	Using Captions	Context Clues	expository descriptive	http://www.peanut-institute.org/PeanutFAQs.html
Q	Mummies, Pyramids, and Pharaohs		Gail Gibbons	Social Studies Nonfiction	Understanding Steps in a Process	Words With Quotations	expository narrative	http://www.cdli.ca/CITE/egypt_activity.htm
Q	Oggie Cooder	Oggie Cooder (#1)	Sarah Weeks	Realistic Fiction	Understanding Making Predictions	Strong Verbs	graphic aid narrative	http://www.guinnessworldrecords.com.
Q	Punished!		David Lubar	Fantasy	Visualizing	Open Syllables	graphic organizer; narrative	http://www.davidlubar.com/teachers.html
Q	You Be the Detective		Marvin Miller	Realistic Fiction	Understanding Problems/Solutions	Compound Words	descriptive expository	http://kids.mysterynet.com/
R	Achoo! The Most Interesting Book You'll Ever Read About Germs	Mysterious You	Trudee Romanek	Informational Text	Understanding Cause and Effect	Silent Letters	expository narrative	http://kidshealth.org/kid/ill_injure/

Level	Title	Series	Author	Genre	Comprehension Strategies	Phonics and Word Study	Writing Options	Technology
R	Island, The		Gary Paulsen	Realistic Fiction	Understanding Setting	Context Clues	expository descriptive	http://www.trelease-on-reading.com/paulsen.html
R	Julian Rodriguez Episode One: Trash Crisis on Earth	Julian Rodriguez	Alexander Stadler	Fantasy	Understanding Point of View	Suffixes	expository list	http://www.njcu.edu/CILL/vol2/sadow.html.
R	More Than Anything Else		Marie Bradby	Historical Fiction	Understanding Character	Personification	descriptive narrative	http://www.nps.gov/bowa/historyculture/the-great-educator.htm
R	Pocahontas and the Strangers		Clyde Robert Bulla	Fictional Biography	Understanding Compare and Contrast	Reading Suffixes	narrative expository	http://www.americaslibrary.gov/cgi-bin/page.cgi/aa/all/pocahonta
R	Report Card, The		Andrew Clements	Fiction	Understanding Theme	Recognizing Synonyms	expository narrative	http://pbskids.org/itsmylife/school/teststress/index.html
R	Rules		Cynthia Lord	Realistic Fiction	Making Predictions	Personification	expository narrative	http://www.autismsource.org/
R	Trumpet of the Swan, The		E.B. White	Fantasy	Recognizing Compare and Contrast	Reading Suffixes	expository narrative	http://www.webenglishteacher.com/white.html
R	Wackiest White House Pets		Kathryn Gibbs Davis	Informational Text	Visualizing	Diphthongs ou, ow	narrative expository	www.presidentialpetmuseum.com/whitehousepets-1.htm
R	When Marian Sang		Pam Muñoz Ryan	Biography	Identifying Problem and Solution	Figurative Language: Metaphor	expository narrative	http://www.library.upenn.edu/exhibits/rbm/anderson
S	4 Kids in 5E & 1 Crazy Year		Virginia Frances Schwartz	Realistic Fiction	Understanding Character	Figurative Language: Similes	graphic organizer; descriptive	http://www.webenglishteacher.com/creative.html
S	Beethoven Lives Upstairs		Barbara Nichol	Historical Fiction	Identifying Cause and Effect	Suffixes -er, -or	letter descriptive	http://www.classicsforkids.com/teachers/lessonplans/beethoven/
S	Bluish		Virginia Hamilton	Realistic Fiction	Drawing Conclusions	Latin Word Roots	descriptive letter	http://kidshealth.org/parent/medical/cancer/cancer_leukemia.html.
S	Dog's Life, A: The Autobiography of a Stray		Ann M. Martin	Fiction	Making Predictions	Word Parts	narrative persuasive	http://www.hsus.org/pets/animal_shelters/
S	Granny Torrelli Makes Soup		Sharon Creech	Realistic Fiction	Understanding Theme	Understanding Idioms	narrative descriptive	http://pbskids.org/itsmylife/friends/friendsfight/article2.html
S	In the Shade of the Nispero Tree		Carmen T. Bernier-Grand	Realistic Fiction	Identifying Plot	Suffixes -ion, -tion, -ation	expository letter	www.timeforkids.com/TFK/teachers/aw/wr/main/0,28132,702661,00.html
S	Let It Begin Here!		Dennis Brindell Fradin	Social Studies Nonfiction	Understanding Historical Content	Unfamiliar Words	graphic aid narrative	www.americanrevolution.com.
S	Million Dollar Shot, The		Dan Gutman	Realistic Fiction	Understanding Plot	Reading Multisyllabic Words	descriptive expository	http://pbskids.org/kws/parentsteachers/
S	Puppies, Dogs, and Blue Northers		Gary Paulsen	Autobiography	Visualizing	Synonyms	expository graphic aid	http://www.iditarod.com/teachers/
S	Tru Confessions		Janet Tashjian	Realistic Fiction	Generating Questions	Context Clues	persuasive expository	http://www.educationworld.com/a_lesson/lesson115.shtml
T	10 Deadliest Plants, The	The 10	Angie Littlefield and Jennifer Littlefield	Science Nonfiction	Categorizing Information	Comparative Adjectives	expository persuasive	http://www.kidsgardening.com
T	Amazing Life of Benjamin Franklin, The		James Cross Giblin	Biography	Uncovering Text Structure	Compound Words	narrative expository	www.teachingbenfranklin.org
T	Chasing Vermeer		Blue Balliett	Realistic Fiction/Mystery	Understanding Plot	Context Clues	graphic aid narrative	www.scholastic.com/blueballiett
T	Dirty Tricks (Raven Hill Mysteries #5)	Raven Hill Mysteries (#5)	Emily Rodda	Mystery	Making Inferences	Suffix -ion	descriptive graphic aid	http://www.mysterynet.com

Level	Title	Series	Author	Genre	Comprehension Strategies	Phonics and Word Study	Writing Options	Technology
T	Drita, My Homegirl		Jenny Lombard	Realistic Fiction	Comparing and Contrasting	Informal Language	graphic organizer/ descriptive; narrative	http://www.nytimes.com/learning/general/specials/kosovo/lessons.html
T	Fair Weather		Richard Peck	Realistic Fiction	Reading Informal Speech	Colloquialisms and Idioms	descriptive letter	http://xroads.virginia.edu/~ma96/WCE/title.html
T	Orphan Train Rider: One Boy's True Story		Andrea Warren	Biography	Identifying Problems and Solutions	Idioms	descriptive narrative	http://www.orphantraindepot.com/
T	Power of Un, The		Nancy Etchemendy	Science Fiction	Understanding Cause and Effect	Prefixes	graphic aid narrative	http://www.pbs.org/wgbh/nova/time/
T	Replay		Sharon Creech	Realistic Fiction	Understanding Theme	Figurative Language	narrative persuasive	http://www2.scholastic.com/browse/collateral.jsp?id=337_type=Contributor_typeId=1811
T	Something Upstairs		Avi	Mystery	Understanding Setting	Difficult Words	expository persuasive	www.kidsreads.com/authors/au-avi.asp
U	Adventures of Marco Polo, The		Russell Freedman	Biography	Understanding Compare and Contrast	Latin Roots	persuasive expository	www.nationalgeographic.com/xpeditions/activities/10/marcopolo.html
U	All of the Above		Shelley Pearsall	Realistic Fiction	Understanding Point of View	Synonyms	narrative expository	http://www.nea.org/neatodayextra/mathfun.html
U	Charlie Bone and the Invisible Boy	Charlie Bone	Jenny Nimmo	Fantasy	Understanding Text Structure	Context Clues	descriptive narrative	http://www.scholastic.com/charliebone/index.htm
U	Creepy Creatures (Goosebumps Graphix)	Goosebumps Graphix (#1)	R.L. Stine	Graphic Novel	Understanding Text Structure	Compound Words	expository narrative	http://www.ncte.org/pubs/chron/highlights/122031.htm
U	Ginger Pye		Eleanor Estes	Realistic Fiction/Mystery	Understanding Characters	Suffixes -er and -est	expository descriptive	http://kclibrary.lonestar.edu/decade50.html
U	Graduation of Jake Moon, The		Barbara Park	Realistic Fiction	Understanding Point of View	Multisyllabic Words	expository narrative	http://www.alz.org/living_with_alzheimers_just_for_kids_and_teens.asp
U	Hush		Jacqueline Woodson	Realistic Fiction	Understanding Plot Sequence	Suffix -ness	expository narrative	http://www.jacquelinewoodson.com/
U	Nothing But the Truth: A Documentary Novel		Avi	Realistic Fiction	Recognizing Events	Colloquialisms	descriptive narrative	www.jiskha.com/social_studies/psychology/rumors.html
U	Tale of Despereaux, The		Kate DiCamillo	Fantasy	Drawing Conclusions	Synonyms	descriptive poetry	http://edsitement.neh.gov/view_lesson_plan.asp?id=387
U	Tangerine		Edward Bloor	Realistic Fiction	Compare and Contrast	Varying Words With Prefixes and Suffixes	narrative expository	http://www2.scholastic.com/browse/collateral.jsp?id=972
V	10 Most Wondrous Ancient Sites, The	The 10	Carol Drake	Social Studies Nonfiction	Using Compare and Contrast	Multisyllabic Words	descriptive persuasive	http://www.wonderclub.com/AllWorldWonders.html
V	Becoming Naomi León		Pam Muñoz Ryan	Realistic Fiction	Understanding Cause and Effect	Suffixes	descriptive narrative	http://www.uwex.edu/ces/gprg/qandas.html#emotion
V	Birdwing		Rafe Martin	Fantasy	Understanding Problem and Solution	Compound Words	narrative descriptive	www.grimmstories.com
V	Desperate Journey		Jim Murphy	Historical Fiction	Generating Questions	Difficult Words	narrative graphic aid	http://www.laguardiawagnerarchive.lagcc.cuny.edu/eriecanal/
V	Ellis Island	Cornerstones of Freedom	Judith Jango-Cohen	Social Studies Nonfiction	Understanding Main Idea and Details	Root Words	expository narrative	www.ellisisland.org/
V	Fall of the Amazing Zalindas, The (Sherlock Holmes/Baker Street Irregulars)		Tracy Mack and Michael Citrin	Mystery	Understanding Character	Context Clues	narrative expository	http://www.kidsloveamystery.com/
V	Firework-Maker's Daughter, The		Philip Pullman	Fairy Tale	Understanding Character	Similes	expository descriptive	www.readwritethink.org/lessons/lesson_view.asp?id=42

Level	Title	Series	Author	Genre	Comprehension Strategies	Phonics and Word Study	Writing Options	Technology
V	Forty Acres and Maybe a Mule		Harriet Robinet	Historical Fiction	Making Predictions	Synonyms	narrative description	www.digitalhistory.uh.edu/reconstruction/index.html
V	Foster's War		Carolyn Reeder	Historical Fiction	Understanding Problems and Solutions	Understanding Strong Verbs	narrative expository	http://teacher.scholastic.com/pearl/
V	Pictures of Hollis Woods		Patricia Reilly Giff	Realistic Fiction	Understanding Point of View	Figurative Language	graphic aid narrative	http://www.bookbrowse.com/biographies/index.cfm?author_number=1073
W	Blood on the River: James Town 1607		Elisa Carbone	Historical Fiction	Drawing Conclusions	Context Clues		www.historyisfun.org/Jamestown-Settlement.htm
W	Chu Ju's House		Gloria Whelan	Realistic Fiction	Visualizing	Suffix -ous	expository descriptive	www.kn.pacbell.com/wired/China/
W	Guilty By a Hair! (24/7: Science Behind the Scenes	24/7: Science Behind the Scenes	Anna Prokos	Science Nonfiction	Noticing Details	Multisyllabic Words	expository graphic aid	http://pbskids.org/dragonflytv/show/forensics.html.
W	Harriet Tubman, Secret Agent		Thomas B. Allen	Social Studies Nonfiction	Generating Questions	Synonyms	expository narrative	http://www.pbs.org/wgbh/aia/part4/title.html
W	Home of the Brave		Katherine Applegate	Free Verse	Understanding Problems and Solutions	Idioms	expository narrative	www.pbs.org/wnet/africa/tools/index.html
W	Invention of Hugo Cabret, The		Brian Selznick	Historical Fiction/Graphic Novel	Understanding Plot	Latin Roots	expository descriptive	http://www.theinventionofhugocabret.com/intro_flash.htm
W	Lightning Thief, The	Percy Jackson (#1)	Rick Riordan	Fantasy	Understanding Visualization	Root Words	persuasive expository	http://www.mythweb.com
W	Lights, Camera, Amalee	Amalee	Dar Williams	Realistic Fiction	Comparing and Contrasting	Prefixes en-, em-	narrative expository	http://www.worldwildlife.org/species/
W	Out From Boneville (Bone)	Bone (#1)	Jeff Smith	Graphic Novel	Understanding Point of View	Nonstandard Spelling	expository narrative	http://www.education-world.com/a_curr/profdev/profdev105.shtml/
W	Tunnels		Roderick Gordon and Brian Williams	Fantasy	Comparing and Contrasting	Colorful Adjectives	narrative expository	http://www2.scholastic.com/browse/collection.jsp?id=300
X	Antarctica: Journeys to the South Pole		Walter Dean Myers	Informational Text	Understanding Text Structure	Understanding Synonyms	narrative expository	http://www.pbs.org/wgbh/nova/shackleton/
X	Break With Charity, A: A Story About the Salem Witch Trials		Ann Rinaldi	Historical Fiction	Understanding Character	Affixes	narrative expository	http://www.law.umkc.edu/faculty/projects/ftrials/salem/salem.htm
X	Fight for Freedom: The American Revolutionary War		Benson Bobrick	Social Studies Nonfiction	Understanding Cause and Effect	Using Context Clues	persuasive expository	http://www.ushistory.org/march/index.html
X	Four Pictures by Emily Carr		Nicolas Debon	Biography/Graphic Format	Making Inferences	Compound Words	narrative expository	www.emilycarr.ca
X	Girl Named Disaster, A		Nancy Farmer	Novel	Visualizing	Similes	poem expository	http://www.pbs.org/wnet/africa/index.html
X	Millicent Min, Girl Genius		Lisa Yee	Realistic Fiction	Understanding Genre	Multiple-Meaning Words	descriptive narrative	http://www.quotationspage.com/subjects/friendship/
X	Somewhere in the Darkness		Walter Dean Myers	Realistic Fiction	Making Predictions	Recognizing Colloquialisms	expository narrative	http://www.readingrockets.org/books/interviews/myersw
X	Storm Thief		Chris Wooding	Science Fiction	Understanding Plot	Antonyms	narrative descriptive	http://www2.ku.edu/_sfcenter/young-SF.htm
X	Usborne Book of Scientists, The: From Archimedes to Einstein		Struan Reid and Patricia Fara	Informational Text	Understanding Cause and Effect	Greek Prefixes tele-, micro-	expository	http://www.intute.ac.uk/sciences/cgi-bin/browse.pl?id=246
X	When Hitler Stole Pink Rabbit		Judith Kerr	Historical Fiction	Identifying Problem/Solution	Adverbs	descriptive graphic aid	http://www.ushmm.org/education
Y	Artemis Fowl (Book 1)	Artemis Fowl (#1)	Eoin Colfer	Fantasy	Identifying Plot	Prefixes com-, con-	expository descriptive	http://edsitement.neh.gov/view_lesson_plan.asp?id=387

Level	Title	Series	Author	Genre	Comprehension Strategies	Phonics and Word Study	Writing Options	Technology
Y	Boy Who Dared, The		Susan Campbell Bartoletti	Historical Fiction	Understanding Theme	Context Clues	narrative persuasive	http://fcit.usf.edu/HOLOCAUST/TIMELINE/timeline.htm
Y	Geronimo: A Novel		Joseph Bruchac	Historical Fiction	Evaluating Author's Purpose	Similes and Metaphors	expository narrative	http://www.indigenouspeople.net/geronimo.htm
Y	Get On Out of Here, Philip Hall		Bette Greene	Realistic Fiction	Identifying Point of View	Suffixes -ation and -ion	letter descriptive	www.activehealthykids.ca/Ophea/Ophea.net/student-youth-leader-ship.cfm
Y	Heroes of the Holocaust: True Stories of Rescues by Teens		Allan Zullo and Mara Bovsun	Social Studies Nonfiction	Understanding Historical Context	Common and Proper Nouns	narrative expository	http://www.adl.org/hidden
Y	Jumping Tree, The		René Saldaña, Jr.	Realistic Fiction	Understanding Character	Context Clues	expository graphic aid	http://nydiabenitez.tripod.com/id24.html
Y	Larklight		Philip Reeve	Science Fiction	Understanding Setting	Metaphors	expository graphic aid	http://www.pbs.org/empires/victoria/ and http://www.victorians.org.uk/
Y	Pemba's Song: A Ghost Story		Marilyn Nelson and Tonya C. Hegamin	Mystery	Understanding Problem and Solution	Colloquialisms	poem graphic aid	http://www.poetryoutloud.org/poems/poet.html?id=80669
Y	Vlad the Impaler: The Real Count Dracula	Wicked History, A	Enid Goldberg and Norman Itzkowitz	Biography	Understanding Historical Context	Context Clues	narrative graphic aid	www.donlinke.com/drakula/vlad.htm
Y	Yearling, The		Marjorie Kinnan Rawlings	Novel	Understanding Structure	Personification	narrative descriptive	www.cah.ucf.edu/crosscreek/rawling1.php
Z	An American Plague		Jim Murphy	Social Studies Nonfiction	Understanding Cause and Effect	Root Words and Affixes	expository narrative	www.philadelphiahistory.org/akm/lessons/yellowFever
Z	Best Ghost Stories Ever, The	Scholastic Classic	Christopher Krovatin	Fiction	Understanding Cause and Effect	Multisyllabic Words	expository narrative	http://people.howstuffworks.com/ghost-stories.htm
Z	Detective Stories		Philip Pullman, editor	Mystery	Drawing Conclusions	Understanding Slang	expository narrative	www.springfieldlibrary.org/stacks/advis.html
Z	Finding My Hat		John Son	Realistic Fiction	Making Inferences	Suffixes	narrative expository	http://www.pbs.org/hiddenkorea/index.htm
Z	Harry Potter and the Deathly Hallows	Harry Potter	J. K. Rowling	Novel	Understanding Chapters	Context Clues	descriptive narrative	http://curriculalessons.suite101.com/article.cfm/harry_potter_lesson_plan
Z	Jane Eyre	Scholastic Classic	Charlotte Brontë	Novel	Understanding Theme	Context Clues	expository persuasive	http://www.haworth-village.org.uk/brontes/charlotte/charlotte.asp
Z	Malcolm X: By Any Means Necessary		Walter Dean Myers	Biography	Identifying Main Idea and Details	Multisyllabic Words	expository persuasive	http://www.cmgww.com/historic/malcolm/about/bio.htm
Z	Stormbreaker (Alex Rider)	Alex Rider Adventure (#1)	Anthony Horowitz	Mystery	Understanding Character	Difficult Words	persuasive narrative	http://www.anthonyhorowitz.com/alexrider/
Z	Time Machine, The		H. G. Wells	Science Fiction	Understanding a Frame Story	Figurative Language: Paradox	narrative descriptive	http://www.mentorplace.org/Future.htm
Z	Toning the Sweep		Angela Johnson	Realistic Fiction	Understanding Point of View	Strong Verbs	expository narrative	http://www.pbs.org/wnet/aaworld/timeline/civil_01.html

GUIDED READING RESEARCH BASE

Essential Element	Key Ideas—National Reading Panel
Phonemic Awareness Instruction in Guided Reading • Children use their beginning connections between letters and sounds to check on their reading. They notice mismatches. They use letter-sound information to know how words begin. • Teachers prompt children to make their reading "look right."	"Phonemic awareness instruction is not a complete reading program; it cannot guarantee the reading and writing success of your students. Long lasting effects depend on the effectiveness of the whole curriculum." (3, p. 9) "Phonemic awareness instruction does not need to consume long periods of time to be effective. In these analyses, programs lasting less than 20 hours were more effective than longer programs." (2, p. 2–6) "In addition to teaching phonemic awareness skills with letters, it is important for teachers to help children make the connection between the skills taught and their application to reading and writing tasks." (2, p. 2–33)
Phonics Instruction in Guided Reading • Teachers select texts that, along with high-frequency words that are available to students, offer opportunities to use phonics skills. • As they introduce texts, support reading, and revisit the text after reading, teachers bring students' attention to features of words and strategies for decoding words. • Students apply word solving strategies to reading continuous texts. • Teachers explicitly demonstrate how to take words apart and apply phonics principles to new words students meet in continuous text. • Teachers explicitly teach phonics principles through word work after the text is read. Word work sessions are connected to a phonics continuum. • Teachers prompt students to use phonics skills to take words apart while reading.	"Children need opportunities to use what they have learned in problem solving unfamiliar words that they encounter within continuous text. They use word solving strategies to take words apart while keeping the meaning in mind." (3, p. 18) "Reading words accurately and automatically enables children to focus on the meaning of text." (3) "Programs should acknowledge that systematic phonics instruction is a means to an end. Some phonics programs focus primarily on teaching children a large number of letter-sound relationships. These programs often do not allot enough instructional time to help children learn how to put this knowledge to use in reading actual words, sentences, and texts. Although children need to be taught the major consonant and vowel letter-sound relationships, they also need ample reading and writing activities that allow them to practice this knowledge." (3, p. 17)
Fluency Instruction in Guided Reading • Texts are selected to be within students' control so that they know most of the words and can read fluently (with teaching). • The teacher introduces the text to support comprehension and connections to language. • Teachers draw students' attention to elements of words that will help them recognize or solve them rapidly.	"If text is read in a laborious and inefficient manner, it will be difficult for the child to remember what has been read and to relate the ideas expressed in the text to his or her background knowledge." (1, p. 22) "Repeated and monitored oral reading improves reading fluency and overall reading achievement." (3, p. 11) "It is important to provide students with instruction and practice in fluency as they read connected text." (3, p. 23) "Word recognition is a necessary but not sufficient condition for fluent reading." (3, p. 30) "Fluency is not a stage of development at which readers can read all words quickly and easily. Fluency changes, depending on what readers are reading, their familiarity with the words, and the amount of their practice with reading text." (3, p. 23)

• Teachers help students to understand and use the language patterns that may be found in written text. • Students use word recognition and comprehending strategies in an orchestrated way while reading or rereading a text silently or orally. • Teachers provide explicit demonstrations and instruction in reading fluency. • Teachers prompt for fluency when students are reading aloud. • Students engage in repeated oral readings to work for fluency.	"By listening to good models of fluent reading, students learn how a reader's voice can help written text make sense." (3, p. 26) "Fluency develops as a result of many opportunities to practice reading with a high degree of success. Therefore, your students should practice orally rereading text that is reasonably easy for them—that is, text containing mostly words that they know or can decode easily." (3, p. 27)
Vocabulary Instruction in Guided Reading • Texts are selected so that students know most of the words but there are a few new words to provide opportunities for learning. • The teacher introduces the text to support comprehension, with specific attention to concepts and words. • Students read the text silently or orally with teacher support. • After reading, students and teacher discuss the meaning of the text, with further discussion of word meanings if needed. • The teacher teaches processing strategies, which may include both word recognition and how to determine word meanings. • Students may extend the meaning of the text through writing, which often includes attention to vocabulary. • The teacher provides 1–2 minutes of pre-planned word work which helps students attend to word parts and word meanings (affixes, word structure, homophones, synonyms, etc.).	"Extended instruction that promotes active engagement with vocabulary improves word learning." (3, p. 36) "Teaching specific words before reading helps both vocabulary learning and reading comprehension." (3, p. 36) "Repeated exposure to vocabulary in many contexts aids word learning." (3, p. 36) "Conversations about books help children to learn new words and concepts and to relate them to their prior knowledge and experience." (3, p. 35) "… the larger the reader's vocabulary (either oral or print), the easier it is to make sense of the text." (1, p. 13) "… children often hear adults repeat words several times. They also may hear adults use new and interesting words. The more oral language experiences children have, the more word meanings they learn." (3, p. 35)
Comprehension Instruction in Guided Reading • Teachers select texts that readers can process successfully with supportive teaching. • The teacher demonstrates effective strategies for comprehending text. • In the introduction to the text, the teacher explains words and concepts and assures that students activate their own prior knowledge. • Students have the opportunity to apply a range of strategies in response to the demands of texts.	"Comprehension is defined as 'intentional thinking during which meaning is constructed through interactions between text and reader' (Harris & Hodges, 1995). Thus, readers derive meaning from text when they engage in intentional, problem-solving thinking processes. The data suggest that text comprehension is enhanced when readers actively relate the ideas represented in print to their own knowledge and experiences and construct mental representations in memory." (1, p. 14) "In general, the evidence suggests that teaching a combination of reading comprehension techniques is the most effective. When students use them appropriately, they assist in recall, question answering, question generation, and summarization of texts. When used in combination, these techniques can improve results in standardized comprehension tests." (1, p. 15) "Text comprehension can be improved by instruction that helps readers use specific comprehension strategies." (2, p. 49)

• Students expand strategies by applying them, with teacher support, to texts that are more difficult than they could read independently. • Teachers help students extend their understandings through using oral language and writing. • Teachers help students extend their understanding through using graphic organizers to understand underlying text structures. • While teachers are working with students in small groups, other students read independently the books that they have previously read.	"Text comprehension can be improved by instruction that helps readers use specific comprehension strategies." (3, p. 9) "Graphic organizers illustrate concepts and interrelationships among concepts in a text, using diagrams or other pictorial devices. Regardless of the label, graphic organizers can help readers focus on concepts and how they are related to other concepts." "Comprehension strategies are not ends in themselves; they are means of helping your students understand what they are reading." (3, p. 6) "Help your students learn to use comprehension strategies in natural learning situations—for example, as they read in the content areas." (3, p. 65) "Readers must know what most of the words mean before they can understand what they are reading." (3, p. 45) "Children learn many new words by reading extensively on their own. The more children read on their own, the more words they encounter and the more word meanings they learn." (3, p. 35) "Teachers not only must have a firm grasp of the content presented in text, but also must have substantial knowledge of the strategies themselves, of which strategies are most effective for different students and types of content and of how best to teach and model strategy use." (1, p. 16)
Motivation Support in Guided Reading • Teachers select books that will be interesting to students. • Teachers introduce texts in a way that engages interest and motivation.	"Few if any studies have investigated the contribution of motivation to the effectiveness of phonics programs, not only the learner's motivation to learn but also the teacher's motivation to teach. The lack of attention to motivational factors by researchers in the design of phonics programs is potentially very serious … Future research should … be designed to determine which approaches teachers prefer to use and are most likely to use effectively in their classroom instruction." (2)
Motivation Support in Guided Reading • Teachers select books that will be interesting to students. • Teachers introduce texts in a way that engages interest and motivation.	"Interesting texts also provide mutual cognitive and motivational benefits (Schiefele, 1999). When students are interested in what they read, they process the material more deeply, gain richer conceptual understandings, and engage more fully with text." (4, p. 416)
Motivation Related to Reading Comprehension • Students who receive motivation support and strategy instruction improve their reading comprehension.	"Motivated students usually want to understand text content fully, and therefore, process information deeply. As they read frequently with these cognitive purposes, motivated students gain in reading proficiency. However, motivation and engagement have rarely been incorporated into experimental studies of instruction or interventions for reading comprehension." (4, p. 403) "(a) Engagement in reading refers to interaction with text that is simultaneously motivated and strategic, (b) engaged reading correlates with achievement in reading comprehension, (c) engaged reading and its constituents (motivation and cognitive strategies) can be increased by instruction practices directed toward them, and (d) an instructional framework that merges motivational and cognitive strategy support in reading will increase engaged reading and reading comprehension." (4, p. 403)

Effect of Engagement on Interest in Reading • Motivated readers are able to monitor their comprehension, recall what they read, and retain and organize the knowledge they gain. • Motivated readers are involved in their reading, often rereading and reflecting on their understanding. • Motivated readers know how reading is relevant to their lives. • Engaged readers find that reading is a meaningful, enjoyable activity.	"…the most highly interested students had positive affect toward books, favored certain authors, and enjoyed favorite topics. These high interest readers typically reread all or portions of books, pursued topics in and out of school, and connected reading to their personal experiences or feelings. Also salient was the students' deep comprehension and complex cognitive command of these texts that accompanied their enjoyment and enthusiasm. Students with high positive affect for a certain topic invariably had deep recollection of information or books about the topic, whereas students with low affect for reading on a topic displayed little recall and grasp of content. This suggests that high interest in reading is not limited to the strong, positive affect surrounding books, but also the high comprehension, recall, and organization of knowledge in memory typical of these readers." (5, p. 13)
Readers' Motivation to Be Responsible for Their Own Learning • Engaged readers are in control of their own learning and are able to express their opinions and their own understandings.	"A substantial proportion of students reported that knowledge and information was what they were seeking in books. We did not create this as a formal construct nor place it in our rubric, because we did not systematically ask all students about the extent that they read for knowledge. However, many students volunteered that they wanted to learn about their favorite topic, enjoyed gaining information, or liked being very well informed in certain domains. Being knowledgeable was an explicit goal mentioned by many, and while it is a commonsense purpose for reading, it has not been formalized quantitatively in prior research as a motivational construct. We believe that reading for the purpose of knowledge development is a vitally important motivational attribute for future investigation." (5, p. 26)
Readers' Engagement With Text • For engaged readers, reading is a highly visual experience as they imagine characters, settings, and events. • Readers who are emotionally engaged in text can often note and understand ideas the author does not explicitly state. • Readers engage in an interchange of ideas between themselves and the text.	"…reading narrative text is often affectively laden, and that readers adopt affective goals for narrative reading. They seek excitement, emotional relationship with characters, interpersonal drama, and a range of aesthetic experiences. Reading information books, in contrast, is energized by goals of reading for knowledge, seeking information, and the desire to explain our physical or cultural worlds. Thus, motivations for reading narrative and information books should be distinguished in studying how motivation develops or how it relates to other factors such as reading comprehension." (5, p. 26-27)
Features of Engaging Classrooms • Engaging classrooms are observational, conceptual, self-directed, strategic, collaborative, coherent, and personalized.	"To increase motivational development, teachers should provide support for situated experiences that increase intrinsic motivation. For example, an exciting activity that may be entertaining, such as reader's theater for a specific book, may increase situated, intrinsic motivation. Likewise, hands-on activities with science materials (a terrarium with plants and animals, or a field trip to a park) or hands-on activities in history (a reenactment of a historical scene within the classroom) will increase situated, intrinsic motivation for texts related to these topics. However, these events will be insufficient to influence long-term motivation for reading. Experimental evidence suggests that increasing generalized intrinsic motivation requires the extended classroom practices of support for students' choices, collaborations, use of interesting texts, and real-world interactions related to literacy." (6, p. 21)

The ideas in this chart are referenced to the following documents:

(1) National Institute of Child Health and Human Development. (2001). *Report of the National Reading Panel: Teaching Children to Read: An Evidence-Based Assessment of the Scientific Research Literature on Reading and Its Implications for Reading Instruction*. Washington, DC: National Institutes of Health.

(2) National Institute of Child Health and Human Development. (2001). *Report of the National Reading Panel: Teaching Children to Read: An Evidence-Based Assessment of the Scientific Research Literature on Reading and Its Implications for Reading Instruction: Report of the Subgroups*. Washington, DC: National Institutes of Health.

(3) Armbruster, B. B., Lehr, F., & Osborn, J. (2001). *Put Reading First: The Research Building Blocks for Teaching Children to Read, Kindergarten through Grade 3*. Washington, DC: U.S. Department of Education.

[i] "Readers must know what most of the words mean before they can understand what they are reading." (*Put Reading First*, p. 45)

[ii] "Beginning readers use their oral vocabulary to make sense of the words they see in print ... Readers must know what most of the words mean before they can understand what they are reading." (*Put Reading First*, p. 45)

(4) Guthrie, John T.; Wigfield, Allan; Barbosa, Pedro, et al., "Increasing Reading Comprehension and Engagement Through Concept-Oriented Reading Instruction," *Journal of Education Psychology*, 2004, Vol. 96, No 3, 403–423.

(5) Guthrie, John T.; Hoa, Laurel W.; Wigfield, Allan; Tonks, Stephen M.; Humneick, Nicole M.; Littles, Erin, "Reading Motivation and Reading Comprehension Growth in the Later Elementary Years," *Contemporary Educational Psychology*, June 3, 2006.

(6) Guthrie, John T.; Hoa, Laurel W.; Wigfield, Allan; Tonks, Stephen M.; Perencevich, Kathleen C., "From Spark to Fire: Can Situational Reading Interest Lead to Long Term Reading Motivation?" *Reading Research and Instruction*, v45, n2, pp. 91–117, Winter 2006, College Reading Association, Brigham Young University, Provo, UT.

BIBLIOGRAPHY

Anderson, E., and Guthrie, J. T. (1999). *Motivating children to gain conceptual knowledge from text: The combination of science observation and interesting texts.* Paper presented at the annual meeting of the American Educational Research Association, Montreal, Canada.

Blevins, Wiley, and Boynton, Alice. "5 Keys to Reading Nonfiction." *The Art of Teaching.* Supplement to *Instructor Magazine*: 4–7.

Brown, H., and Cambourne, B. (1987). *Read and retell: A strategy for the whole-language/natural learning classroom.* Portsmouth, NH: Heinemann.

Chall, J. S. (1983). *Stages of reading development.* New York: McGraw-Hill.

Clay, M. M. (1993). *Reading Recovery: A Guidebook for Teachers in Training.* Portsmouth, NH: Heinemann.

Dreher, M. J. (2000). Fostering reading for learning. In L. Baker, M. J. Dreher & J. Guthrie (Eds.), *Engaging young readers: Promoting achievement and motivation* (pp. 94–118). New York: Guilford.

Duke, Nell K., and Bennett-Armistead, V. Susan (2003). *Reading & Writing Informational Text in the Primary Grades: Research-Based Practices.* New York, NY: Scholastic Inc.

Gibson, Akimi, Gold, Judith, and Sgouras, Charissa. (2003). "The Power of Story Retelling." *The Tutor.* Spring 2003.

Fountas, Irene, and Pinnell, G. S. (1996). *Guided Reading: Good First Teaching for All Children.* Portsmouth, NH: Heinemann.

Fountas, Irene, and Pinnell, G. S. (2001). *Guiding Readers and Writers, Grades 3–6.* Portsmouth, NH: Heinemann.

Fountas, Irene, and Pinnell, G. S., eds. (1999). *Voices on Word Matters.* Portsmouth, NH: Heinemann.

Jobe, R., & Dayton-Sakari, M. (2002). *Infokids: How to use nonfiction to turn reluctant readers into enthusiastic learners.* Markham, Ontario, Canada: Pembroke.

Kamil, M. L., & Lane, D. M. (1998). Researching the relation between technology and literacy: An agenda for the 21st century. In D. R. Reinking, L. D. Labbo, M. McKenna, & R. Kieffer (Eds.), *Literacy for the 21st century: Technological transformations in a post-typographic world* (pp. 235–251). Mahwah, NJ: Erlbaum.

Pinnell, Gay Su, and Fountas, I. C. (1999). *Matching Books to Readers: A Leveled Book List for Guided Reading, K–3.* Portsmouth, NH: Heinemann.

Pinnell, Gay Su, and Fountas, I. C. (1998). *Word Matters: Teaching Phonics and Spelling in the Reading/Writing Classroom.* Portsmouth, NH: Heinemann.

Pinnell, G. S., Pikulski, J. J., Wixson, K. K., Campbell, J. R., Gough, R. B., and Beatty, A. S. (1995). *Listening to Children Read Aloud: Data from NAEP's Integrated Reading Performance Record (IPRR) at Grade 4.* Report No. 23-FR-04 Prepared by Educational Testing Service under contract with the National Center for Education Statistics, Office of Educational Research and Improvement, U.S. Department of Education. (p. 15)

Venezky, R. L. (1982). The origins of the present-day chasm between adult literacy needs and school literacy instruction. *Visible Language, 16,* 112–127.

RESEARCH AND VALIDATION

A strong pattern of rising scores has been found in schools where daily guided reading has been combined with phonics and word study mini-lessons and daily writing workshops. For further information, see:

Williams, Jane. (2002). The power of data utilization in bringing about systemic school change. *Mid-Western Educational Researcher,* 15, 4–10.

Williams, E. J., Scharer, P., & Pinnell, G. S. (2000). *Literacy Collaborative 2002 Research Report.* Columbus, OH: The Ohio State University.

Scharer, P., Williams, E. J., & Pinnell, G. S. (2001). *Literacy Collaborative 2001 Research Report.* Columbus, OH: The Ohio State University.